SMART RETAIL

Smart Retail

Winning ideas and strategies from the most successful retailers in the world

RICHARD HAMMOND

Vice President, Publisher: Tim Moore
Associate Publisher and Director of Marketing: Amy Neidlinger
Acquisitions Editor: Megan Graue
Operations Specialist: Jodi Kemper
Assistant Marketing Manager: Megan Graue
Cover Designer: Alan Clements
Managing Editor: Kristy Hart
Project Editor: Jovana San Nicolas-Shirley
Proofreader: Sarah Kearns
Senior Compositor: Gloria Schurick
Manufacturing Buyer: Dan Uhrig

Publishing as FT Press

Upper Saddle River, New Jersey 07458

Authorized adaptation from the original UK edition, entitled *Smart Retail, Third Edition*, by Richard Hammond, published by Pearson Education Limited, ©Pearson Education 2011.

This U.S. adaptation is published by Pearson Education, Inc.,

FT Press offers excellent discounts on this book when ordered in quantity for bulk purchases or special sales. For more information, please contact U.S. Corporate and Government Sales, 1-800-382-3419, corpsales@pearsontechgroup.com. For sales outside the U.S., please contact International Sales at international@pearson.com.

Printed in the United States of America

First Printing May 2012

ISBN-10: 0-13-306612-6

ISBN-13: 978-0-13-306612-8

Pearson Education LTD.
Pearson Education Australia PTY, Limited.
Pearson Education Singapore, Pte. Ltd.
Pearson Education Asia, Ltd.
Pearson Education Canada, Ltd.
Pearson Educación de Mexico, S.A. de C.V.
Pearson Education—Japan
Pearson Education Malaysia, Pte. Ltd.

The Library of Congress cataloging-in-publication data is on file.

Smart
Retail

. . . is still dedicated to customers—the people who pay our wages.
Source: Koworld

Contents

Part four   Store

Make it brilliant and they will spend.

Acknowledgments

56 421315 >

Thank you so much to all the retailers and friends who so kindly gave me your help—it's all been so valuable. Thanks especially to Mark, Steve, Nick, Chris, Kevin, TT, John, Jim, and Rocky who have been there with ideas, suggestions, and the offer of a beer many times when the going has been tough.

A retail career takes us away from our family and friends for huge chunks of time. To be a retailer is impossible without the patience of the people we love. I have been so lucky to have a wonderful family support me in all those twists and turns that a life in retail offers. To Rosy, Isabella, Bump, and Emily—thank you so much for being awesome.

I would like to say a special "thank you" to those inspirational friends who have made retail so rewarding for me. First, to Umesh Vadodaria and Mahendra Patel for making me get off my bum and do things. To "Buffalo" Steve Smith for that very first break at 16. To Glyn Moser for making me see how important people are. To Janet for the belief that I could get the things in my head out and down on paper. To Rachael Stock at Pearson for making the original edition of this book better than I had imagined it could be. Thank you also to all the many retailers who gave up time, advice, and ideas for *Smart Retail*—you know who you are and you are all superstars.

I would like to add this last thing: all the effort, sacrifice, setbacks, and challenges have been worth it. Retail is the best life in the world.

Photo Acknowledgments

The publisher would like to thank the following for kind permission to reproduce their photographs:

A&P Historical Society: p. 195; **(c) National Portrait Gallery, London:** p. 203; **GNU Free Documentation License: Wikipedia:** Bobak Ha'Eri p. 201; **Koworld:** p. 3, p. v, p. 23, p. 44, p. 70, p. 124, p. 146, p. 182, p. 208; **MPREIS:** Thomas Jantscher p. 149; **Press Association Images:** p. 197, Herbert Proepper p. 199; **RIBA Library Photographs Collection:** p. 192; **Steve Bowbrick:** p. 89; **US Patent Office:** p. 194

Every effort has been made to trace the copyright holders and we apologize in advance for any unintentional omissions. We would be pleased to insert the appropriate acknowledgment in any subsequent edition of this publication.

Introduction to this Edition

How to get the best from *Smart Retail*

Smart Retail is written from an enterprising store manager's perspective—I've done that to make it easier to read but I want to be clear that whatever your role in retail, there is a lot to gain from giving the thing a read. In Appendix I are notes specific to various job roles: Take a look at them before you plunge into the main sections, of which there are four:

1 **You**—*personal tips for honing your retail eye.*

2 **Team**—*how to get the best from your people.*

3 **Customer**—*how to delight them.*

4 **Store**—*getting the environment right.*

Each section can be read in any order, or even on its own. You might want to start with whichever area you feel needs most work. It is fair to say that I believe most solutions to retail challenges can be found from within the team, which is why the "Team" section makes up such a big part of the book.

Above all, this is a working book. I invite you to flick through, to cherry-pick the bits that suit you best, scribble on the pages, tear stuff out, and share it. If I ever came into your store, I would love to see that your copy of the book has a broken spine, page corners turned down, a forest of Post-it notes sticking out the top, and coffee stains on the cover.

Preface—Why retailing?

One thing that hasn't changed is that retail is still physically and mentally hard work. The pressure's always on; we're only ever as good as our last trading day. Every time we open the store, what follows could be a disaster or a triumph.

And that's the thrill of the thing, that's why we do it—get things right, get the team pulling together, make customers happy, and take some money ... well, those are the days that keep us coming back for more. Getting retail right is thrilling—magic, even.

> **Getting retail right is thrilling—magic, even.**

Welcome then to *Smart Retail,* where together we can try to make sure that you enjoy more good days, better profits, a happier team, an improved business performance, and a boost to your retail career. I love selling things in shops, it is my passion, and this book is all about sharing retail excellence so that we can all enjoy the good bits of that more often.

That there Internet thing

Selling online has had a massive impact on what we do and it is an impact that will continue to grow, not just through e-commerce but in how easily-available information and price-comparision forces change in the way retail works overall. Nowhere in the book though do I make much distinction between retailing on the Internet and retailing in a store—and that's because they are the *same* activity. Both forms are about selling products people want in nice, shoppable, environments—supported by robust systems, great customer service, and effective communications. Retail standards apply in the same way across both.

Where distinctions do apply is in the suitability of your product, positioning, and format to either form. The rule of thumb is this: If you are a bricks-and-mortar retailer then you are unwise to be without a credible online outlet—it's another store and one with a big potential catchment area. The other way around though and it's less clear-cut: The Internet allows smaller retailers to reach far more people, more directly, and more powerfully than a few physical stores might.

As Internet retailing has matured, so too has an acceptance that both forms can learn from each other. Internet retailers have begun to understand better the principles of the complete customer experience, while bricks-and-mortar retailers have slowly begun to learn how to communicate better and how to give customers more reasons to come back. Reminding us that they exist, telling us about good things we might like to buy, and reminding us to come visit is something the best Internet retailers do superbly well—better than any high-street store. Internet retailers say "thank you" better than traditional ones too and that's more powerful than you might think.

Asking the questions

Each edition of *Smart Retail* has been put together on the back of a simple question that I've asked the world's best retailers: "What makes you so good?" Maybe it's a surprise that they would reveal the answer to that question? That they have, over and over to me, is, I think, because great retailers have a passion not just for their own success but a determination that the more retail businesses out there who get retail right then the better off we all become. A vibrant retail sector plays a critical role in the success of economies and, as it goes, the UK in particular owes much of its last decade of success to the superb performance of some of the best retail businesses on the planet. Equally, when customers stop spending ... 2009 and 2010 were tough: We lost a few businesses but others strengthened and learned. I've experienced three recessions in 25 years of retailing now and I'm sure I'll experience future ones too. We push through and we survive by continuing to give customers what they want, need, and didn't know they were looking for.

Is it rocket science?

Because the book is founded on examples of best practice and because, as we will explore later, there are few "new tricks" in retail: Much of what we cover has been done before; I make no secret of that. You will already know lots of it and you will easily understand all of it. This isn't a bullshit fairy-dust consultants" book: This is a collection of answers to your challenges; it is a professional self-help resource—it's not about doing the impossible and being one of the tiny handful of people who invent something new; it's about helping you to make the best use of your own retail instincts and to benefit from the experiences of others.

Brass tacks

The essence of *Smart Retail* is about helping you to make more money, to win the sales battle, and to help you and your team stand out from the competition.

Stars of the shop floor

A good store manager can make a huge impact on the success of an individual store, much more so than a clever marketing director or number-lovin" finance chief can. With a good manager at the helm, great sales teams can make a big and immediate impact. Although I've presented the ideas here in straightforward terms, that doesn't mean they're not sophisticated: We're talking about best practice learned from time spent with the world's best retailers—everything here is accessible to store teams and everything is potentially incredibly powerful.

Much as I'd love the bosses to use *Smart Retail* to make positive changes, I'm hoping that grafters out there on the shop floor will read it too. I've had a lot of feedback from so-called "lowly" checkout people and sales assistants who have been inspired by *Smart Retail* to push themselves forward. So much for "lowly"—I'm really looking forward to the day when my agency is ringing you ex-checkout people and asking if we can come and work for you in your retail empires. It's been fun writing this edition but if just one more person, maybe you, uses the book to realize their true retail potential, well, that's worth more than gold to me.

That gives me masses of hope for your success too. There is nothing to stop you pushing yourself—good ideas, retail ability, and energy are valuable—use the ideas and strategies in *Smart Retail* to make the breakout and to create momentum for yourself.

At the risk of this all going a bit Tony Robbins, you can do it!

PART ONE—**YOU**

Starting at the beginning.

Choose your own direction.
Source: Koworld

1

CHAPTER ONE

What do you want for yourself?

Why do you come to work? It's a cold wintry morning in a small town and you've got a store to open, a cash register to man, or a desk to get to. Why do you bother? It's an important question—it's worth thinking about and worth taking a grown-up look at the answers.

Whatever the specific answers, there's likely to be in there things like: our desire to feel good about ourselves through being good at stuff, to create a little security for our kids, to give our partners reasons to be proud of us, even material things like wanting enough money for a nice house or a great car—or to get enough cash together to stop working for a bit. All of that is good—what's important is that we be honest with ourselves. Once you work out why you're really hauling yourself into city center in the dark of a December morning—then you have a chance to understand how to get the best out of that day, the next week, and the next year.

It's a simple human thing: If I want a nice house I've got to earn money, if I've got to earn money I need to have a good job, if I'm going to have a good job then I need to perform and get noticed, if I'm going to get noticed then I need to do the numbers, if I'm going to do the numbers then I have to keep my team and customers happy ... you can keep this process winding back all the way to the one small thing—maybe something you hate doing—that you need to do right now, right after you've had five minutes of reading this. That small thing you do next—that's earning you that nice house. It is.

This process, this way of thinking, doesn't just apply to material stuff: Let's say your personal goal is a creative one, the work you do, the nasty bits in particular, can be linked, by stepping back this way, to getting your play written, or to quitting retail to go to art school, or whatever. There

Give the best you can to get the thing you want.

is pride to be had in grafting in retail in order to use the results of that graft to move you forward toward a non-retail goal. Give the best you can to get the thing you want. Simple stuff.

Action-planning means doing stuff

Most action planning is a load of old trash—action plans and reality are rarely aligned. It's simple v. complex: A good action plan is one that starts with a goal and then steps back from that goal, practical-step-by-practical-step, until it arrives at the very next thing you must do to move things along.

But just thinking about what you want to achieve is useless without a practical plan: I was taught the techniques of visioning by legendary trainer Bob Caton, and his practical technique is a cracker. Bob is more content with life than pretty much anyone I've ever met. His favorite visioning story is of the house he built for himself in Thailand—he bought a patch of land as soon as he could afford to and then every night at home in England, imagined himself sitting on the veranda at a house that didn't exist. He would describe to himself how it would feel, the taste of the cold beer in his mouth, the warmth of the breeze on his arms, the comfort of the chair, and so on. Then in the morning, he would picture the house once again, and this time he would run a very fast step-back from the beer on the veranda and right to the things he needed to do that day, like call a prospect or get on a 6:45 a.m. train. Two things happened for Bob—he felt better about things he wasn't all that keen on having to do and he got his house built.

So it's not just the end-goal that you think about—it's all those steps that link from there back to the right now. Here's a simplified rundown of Bob's vision:

▶ I want that first ice-cold beer on the veranda of my own house in Thailand.

▶ I need to build that house.

▶ I need to have the plans drawn up.

▶ I need to have the funds in place.

▶ My business needs to have been successful enough to generate x profit over y years.

▶ That means I need to have taught an average of xxx days training per year.

▶ Which would have come from three permanent clients and ten casual contracts.

▶ To hit those numbers, I need to have pitched nine major projects and developed one hundred good prospects.

▶ That means x phone calls and y letters over z period.

▶ I need to write four letters and make six calls today.

Of course, there are also technical steps I've left out for expediency such as understanding what you're selling, commissioning marketing material, and so on. You need to include all that in your plan. But you get the idea—it shows how the grind today, right now, can get you something cool and important in your life.

One of the best things you can do to get yourself motivated is to read Prof. Richard Wiseman's excellent *59 Seconds* (Macmillan, 2009)—in the motivation chapter, he'll tell you all about where visioning can go wrong and how to stop that from happening. He'll also tell you how things like sharing your goals make a provable difference to achieving them.

I'm not about to turn into some hokey self-help twonk here and ask you to stand on your chair and shout "I can." All I'm asking is for the moment's hesitation before rejecting an idea and for you to couple that to achieving your own personal ambitions.

At its simplest, all this is about being open to achieve things, being slower with "no," "impossible," and "just can't happen," and quicker with "let's find out," "let's try it." Thinking this way clears the path to achieving your personal goals.

Raw passion makes us great

All the best retailers are naturally passionate about their businesses. I would suggest it's the one single thing that unites them—without passion, you cannot achieve long-term success in retail. Sure, loads of other skills are important: leadership, an eye for product, team-building, accounting, service, and design. But all of these can to a greater or lesser extent be learned from a book. If you are weak in one or two of these areas you can still usually get by. But without passion, you just won't make a life in retail work for you.

Passion is what drives great retail; and customers, as well as colleagues, love it.

Passion is what drives great retail; and customers, as well as colleagues, love it. Passion is the magic ingredient that helps you to bring surprise, drama, great service, exciting products, and delight into the store.

Customers leave a store run by a passionate team feeling like they want to come back. The team looks forward to coming into work, knowing that today might be the day to break some records, have some fun, and create something great. You could be a cashier at ASDA or the head honcho at Target—as long as you feel that passion, the retail world is your oyster.

Passion to make things better

Passion is not about sales; it is about improvement. Mahendra Patel is one of the finest passionate retailers I've ever met. MP, as we all know him, worked most of his retail life as a store manager and then as a senior field manager. Before that, MP was a teacher in Uganda. In 1973, MP and his family had to flee for their lives in the wake of Ide Amin's murderous purge of the Ugandan Asian population. Arriving in the UK with nothing had, as you would expect, a deep impact on Mahendra. Many people would sink. MP didn't; he started out all over again, this time as a sales assistant in a Dixons store. After more than a quarter of a century in stores, and his having gone through so much, I couldn't understand why the ultra laid-back Mahendra always refused the offers of promotion into head office that regularly came his way (including one invite, I remember, that included a retail CEO sending down the company jet to bring MP back for lunch and a chat). He could have been running the whole show, I would often, exasperated, tell him. I'll admit that I began to question where exactly Mahendra's passion was.

Then over a meal one evening, Mahendra told me: "I am a teacher, I always was. My job is to make as many people as I possibly can feel that they can be better than they are now, that they can improve their lot. Life is about hope and I've been lucky enough to give some of the people who have worked with me some of that hope."

I don't think I ever saw MP actually sell anything, but his stores, and regions, always performed better when he was at the helm. MP's passion was for improvement: not to create teams of sales animals but to make things better—better for colleagues and better for customers. That passion is what makes this retail business great.

CHAPTER TWO

Rising above the crowd

So, passion, then, is massively important but so is being able to direct that passion into achieving stuff. Part of the challenge is getting yourself noticed—showing the wider business that you are a bit special and a person worth backing. I'm specifically talking here to those of you grafting inside a big retailer: If you work for, say, Tesco, you would be a single voice among 148,000 colleagues. If you are going to accelerate your career, or you just want to get good ideas heard, acted upon, and producing benefits for the whole business, then you have to raise your profile in the company. You have to become the one in 148,000 that everybody notices.

You have to become the one in 148,000 that everybody notices.

These are my top suggestions for raising your profile in a multiple-store environment.

Volunteer for things

Put your name forward for projects at all levels. You hear that your area manager wants someone to look after a roll-out? Stick your hand up for that one. Help open new stores, get onto special projects by volunteering for them every time. Getting involved will bring you into contact with senior members of the team, who value and appreciate the help. Such projects often turn out to be good fun and hard work but a nice break from the normal routine.

Introduce yourself to people at every meeting

Go up to the marketing director at the next annual conference and say "hello." Tell him or her who you are and where you work. If you have a useful point to make about the business or the presentations you have seen at the conference, even better. Try not to corner them though—or you'll get a reputation for being a bit scary.

Make good use of the ideas program if there is one

If there's a proper ideas program in place, use it. Put clear sensible ideas into the program whenever you can. Make each submission separately— that way you increase your chance of the evaluation committee noticing you. Offer to help apply the idea too.

Give people your cell phone number

Whenever a senior person comes into your store, engage them. Give them your cell phone number and mention that you are always happy to have them bounce ideas off you. The best people at head office know the value of having people in stores they can turn to for "reality checks" on ideas and projects.

Form an opinion

If you have something interesting and cohesive to say, that will help you to appear more credible when you introduce yourself to senior people. Don't be afraid to research and then to rehearse an opinion. Both those things help to make you worth talking to.

Specialize

Become an expert in a particular area, especially one in which you have experience.

Become an expert in a particular area, especially one in which you have experience. Read up on that subject, start to bring it into conversations, and let people know that you are an information source and that you are happy to share your knowledge.

Produce the goods

Success does your talking for you: In whatever role you occupy, make sure that you are delivering the very best possible performance. That's what this book is for: to give you lots of ways in which to meet and exceed your targets.

CHAPTER THREE
Keeping it simple

Selling stuff in shops is incredibly straightforward. It's not easy—easy and hard are different things to simple and complex—but it is straightforward. You'll come across retail businesses all the time that tie themselves in knots of complexity, you might even work for one of them, and it almost always leads to eventual disaster.

Equally, retailing isn't about inventing brand-new ways of doing things, have a look in the "History" section in Chapter 16 and you'll see that there have only ever been four genuine innovations in retail history. That's liberating: You don't have to be the fifth person in history to come up with something brand new to be a great retailer. Rather it's about creatively applying simple principles: like understanding who might want to buy the stuff you'd like to sell; working out where they might like to do that; and presenting a shop that gets them all excited about being in it.

The world's best retailers all, without exception, do "simple" brilliantly: They communicate simple ideas clearly and quickly and they meet obvious straightforward needs in simple, straightforward, ways. You want a cheap T-shirt—you go to Primark; you want a tasty and fresh sandwich—you go to Pret A Manger; you want honest help and advice—you go to John Lewis.

Brilliant retail businesses do "simple" brilliantly: They make it clear what they are for, they sort things out, they make things happen through heavy application of common sense and "the obvious." It pains me to see retailers drag their businesses through horribly complex processes of organizational change, branding transformation, and culture-shifting without really understanding the common-sense issues and without having a clue who their customers are. And it happens all the time.

Case study 3.1 Not Smart Retail: Woolworths doesn't understand you anymore

Blimey, but the Woolworths story upsets me: thousands of dedicated staff out of a job, lots of suppliers with a big hole in their accounts, a great heritage lost and, worst of all, loads of communities suddenly missing a really important retailer from their local towns. Why was Woolies important? Because it was a great place for lots of us to get all those nice little treats and sundries without having to get in the car or on the bus to get out of town, it was cheap—we could afford to get the kids a toy there, we could afford a can of paint to make the house look a bit nicer, we could do simple and easy things in simple and easy ways without busting our budgets.

The reality is that Woolworths officially blamed their demise on Tesco and Primark having better buying power than they had themselves. I don't think this is quite right. Woolworths over-complicated their business, forgot who their customers were, and stopped giving real people what they actually needed. And the proof of that hypothesis? Simply that Woolworths isn't really dead at all—their customers found a new Woolworths that under-stood them better, and it's called Wilkinsons. Wilkinsons swiped Woolies" lunch from right under the noses of Woolworths senior management.

I can remember sitting down with one of the Woolies marketing team a few years back and damn-near screaming at him to stop waiting for consultants to give him profiles of his "six magic customer types" and instead go talk to staff and customers in some of his shops. To go talk to the people walking past his stores and to ask them what they loved and hated about Woolworths. Ask them what they want, what they liked about his rivals. To get to know them in the simplest way possible: by talking to them face-to-face. Now, this chap is a nice guy but he just didn't get it and so he and similarly minded colleagues ran one of Britain's best-loved stores off the edge of a cliff. It was unforgivable and, yes, I'm angry. Angry for those staff, suppliers, and customers who have lost out. Old tough and gnarly F.W. Woolworth himself would be in tears, he really would.

It didn't need to happen. A Woolworths that went back to its roots, that talked and listened to its customers and store staff would have pulled itself around. Probably after some drastic change, sure, to pare things back as Woolworths did in the 1980s under the wise stewardship of Sir Geoff Mulchay, a man who never has lost touch with real people and real needs. But it would have succeeded—Wilkinsons proves that.

Talk is cheap but it's worth lots

I mentioned talking to store staff there, and can't stress enough how crucial that is: No matter how hard you try, the cleaner in your lowest-profile store knows your business and your customers better than you do. So, talk to them and learn—you'll run the company better if you do.

You've all heard the acronym KISS, right? "Keep It Simple Stupid." It's advice I often get from my mate Kevin McNally at Sony during his briefings. It's good advice too—forcing you to come back to the basic truths of any given situation.

Retail is simple things—simple principles, strongly executed. Those principles are about human things. And that's what this book is about—reconnecting with the human, the simple, the foundation stuff that retail is really all about. We're not going to chuck out the numbers but we most certainly are going to learn how to use them to our advantage as proper emotion-driven retailers.

If we do this, we will achieve more success—the evidence within the world's best retailers proves that time and time again. Carphone Warehouse, amazon.com, Wal-Mart, Tesco, IKEA—they don't complicate, they simplify: They get on with things and they make huge amounts of money.

4

Rolling those snowballs

You'll get fed up of reading me declare that there are no secrets to retail, so I thought I ought to chuck at least one sort-of-secret into the pot early doors: It's the one about change. Rather than having to unlock some massive total change to improve your business, the secret is to recognize that lots of small changes are just as useful. Retail is about trying things: constantly adapting, nudging, and improving parts of the store. Sometimes you *will* do that all at once, when creating a new format, but most of the time it's small changes strung together that result in big improvements.

One thing changed can be the start of something big. Change one detail noticed by one customer, who mentions it to five others, who each tell five more, and you can see that one change can make a big impact. Your team too begins to see things starting to happen, just from one idea. Employee attitudes begin to improve. Baby steps: Do one thing brilliantly today, another tomorrow, and maybe change the world next week. Remember rolling snowballs as a kid? It's like that; you start small and with a bit of effort you soon have something big going on.

> **Baby steps: Do one thing brilliantly today, another tomorrow, and maybe change the world next week.**

Case study 4.1 Not Smart Retail: Observation, change, and simplicity

In the last edition of this book, I had a case study here about an anonymous retailer that included this quote:

▶

This business tries to solve that problem [of not understanding their customers] by trundling off down incredibly twisty consultancy roads and arriving, more lost than ever, at crazy conclusions. The one thing they never do? Stand in their stores and watch who comes in. They never talk to their customers face-to-face. Conversations on the spur of the moment can tell you so much. Detailed research is important and is useful but it's no replacement for pounding the shop floor (in your competitors' stores as well as your own) and talking to people.

Well, I can safely reveal now that the anonymous retailer went bust and that it was Woolworths in the UK. You've read earlier how angry I am (as are plenty of others) that the senior management there were so deaf to the obvious. So you don't suffer the same fate, the following is probably the simplest but most powerful store-assessment tool you'll ever use. It's about looking, listening, and doing, and it's incredibly easy to do all the time.

Reading stores the practical way

Regularly run this assessment of your own store but also of competitors and non-competitors alike—you'll uncover loads of ideas and possibilities each time you do. There are three areas to observe:

A—The store
B—Its staff
C—Its customers

A—Store

I'll bet good money that you already do this when you walk into a shop: you look around. You look at the fixtures, the offers, the dirt on the carpet, and you spot the display gaps. You might even see those gaps and suck your teeth a bit and feel relieved that some other manager is under pressure for once.

Start outside the store—over the road if possible:

▶ Watch people walking past.

▶ How many glance at the window?

▶ How do they react if they do?

▶ How do they move if they then come into the store?

Now find a place inside to stand still and observe:

▶ Watch where customers are going.

▶ Which part of each section do they enter first?

▶ Look at people's eyes.

    ▶ What do they see?

    ▶ What do they miss?

▶ What things do they touch?

    ▶ Which items do they pick up and from where?

    ▶ How long do customers linger over each display fixture?

▶ How many lookers at each display take something to the counter, or to the changing room?

▶ What sorts of people are shopping the store? Moms with strollers, office workers, or mechanics? (This profile will be different at different times of the day.)

▶ Pay special regard to what happens in the transition zone, that area near the door that transfers customers from the outside and then into the store—how do people move through this area?

Most of us make a really basic mistake when we shop our own store. We tend to look at it from back to front. We usually see the store from the back staff area or warehouse through the shopfloor and out of the front doors. It's a natural mistake but incredibly unhelpful. We just aren't seeing the store in the way our customers do.

Then take a look at the basic store components, including:

▶ Window displays

▶ Promotions

▶ Range

- ▶ Pricing logic
- ▶ Fixtures and fittings
- ▶ Lighting layouts
- ▶ Added-value ideas

Make a special note of the bits of the store in which a lot of customers seem to be picking stuff up—that physical interaction is one of your best starts to converting a browse into a sale. What is it that you've done in these areas that customers seem to be reacting to?

Go through this in your competitors' stores and in other stores that interest you too. I believe firms should not only encourage you to go out reading your competitors' stores but they should even give you a paid session, every week, to go off and do so. In fact, they should even give you a fiver to go get a latte to slurp while you walk around improving your business through learning from your competitors and other retailers.

B—Staff

Talk to staff every time you go into a shop. An easy icebreaker is to ask "What's it like working here?" You will usually get a plain answer along the lines of "It's not too bad," which doesn't tell you much but does give you a chance to then ask "What do you like about it?" Nearly every time you ask that, the assistant will let slip a nugget of useful information:

- ▶ "There's a nice team spirit."
- ▶ "The pay is good."
- ▶ "It's a laugh."
- ▶ "We're treated with a bit of respect."
- ▶ "Every day is different."
- ▶ "I like customers."

Each of those answers allows you to unobtrusively ask further questions that help to get to specific employment practices in play at that store. Try to chat with the store manager too. Tell them what you do. Share some thoughts and ideas with them and they often will with you.

C—Customers

Listen:

▶ What do customers say to each other?

▶ What do they say to assistants?

▶ How are customers being approached?

Talking to customers in your own store is easy: You've got a badge on that says you are okay to talk to. Talking to customers elsewhere is a bit harder to do. We tend to be a little wary of strangers asking questions but it can be done without you appearing to be a crazy person. Most people do love to share their opinions—turn that to your advantage.

> **Most people do love to share their opinions—turn that to your advantage.**

In your own store, you can ask lots of open questions such as:

▶ "How well have we looked after you today?"

▶ "What do you think about how we've changed our displays?"

▶ "How easy was it to find what you were looking for?"

▶ "What do you think of these new products?"

▶ "How easy is it to shop in my store?"

▶ "What was the first thing you noticed when you came in today?"

▶ "What's your opinion on how I've set up my register area?"

▶ "What am I missing in my store, do you think?"

▶ "What sort of things do other shops like mine do that you really like?"

When I'm in my plainclothes and out in somebody else's store, I find the most successful question tends to be "I run a store like this one; what do you like about this shop?" and I'll be asking that usually while waiting in a line at the checkout. Lots of other opportunities to open up a conversation usually present themselves while wandering around the store too.

If the customer starts to chat happily, be conversational and don't try to sound like you're doing a survey. People tend to respond along the lines of "Oh, I like the way they do X but I really wish they would sort out that damn Y." Maybe we just like complaining but I have found over and over again that these little chats can uncover a glaring problem for you to look out for in your own store. Of course, some customers will also happily give you a rundown of what it is that attracts them to the particular store you are in, and that's extra useful.

Street Time

As a consultancy we do a cracking version of exactly this process: We send teams of senior retailers, each clutching a twenty, out into shops. We call this program "Street Time" and those retailers are targeted with visiting a selected set of stores and reporting back on them. They talk to staff (we've had at least a dozen staff hired by our clients after having had great in-store conversations), they talk to customers, and occasionally they get escorted out by over-zealous security guards. The most useful part is always, they tell us, the standing back and watching customers bit—we give ourselves that essential time too infrequently.

You'll find the very simple notes for our Street Time exercise in Appendix III—read the sections on Big Idea, Discovery, and Mission before taking a crack at it.

Turning the things we see into things we do

Reading stores is powerful only if you do it with a purpose. That purpose is to find one thing to change in your own store or business today. Write down your notes as soon as you can and then do a bit of simple analysis: set up three headings "benefit," "effort" and "cost." Mark each idea out of ten for each of those headings and then pick out the ones that look most attractive and get on with them!

All of these you would consider doing:

▶ Lots of benefit, easy to do, no cost

▶ Useful benefit, easy to do, no cost

▶ Lots of benefit, bit of effort required, some cost

▶ Useful benefit, bit of effort required, some cost

These you would not do:

▶ Some benefit, easy to do, lots of cost
▶ Little benefit, hard to do, lots of cost

PART TWO—**TEAM**

Make us happy and we will make you money.

Source: Koworld

5

CHAPTER FIVE

What's the Big Idea?

The most important bit in the whole book is this part. Big Idea: Knowing what the hell you actually are; this is the absolute foundation stone of a great retail business. Once you work out what you are, you can get really good at being that thing and get really good at telling people what that thing is and why they might like it: You can build a store that people want to come to and spend money in because they explicitly understand what you're giving them.

Every great retail business is built around a Big Idea—a reason for existing, the thing that business is for; it informs absolutely everything that the retailer does and says, and informs every decision made within it. It is the starting point for everything in the business. I've put it in this section of the book because it has a big impact on the team—you can recruit, motivate, and inspire people around a great Big Idea.

Every great retail business is built around a Big Idea.

Big Idea is the thing that has Hotel Chocolat growing and, for the want of a Big Idea, has Thorntons shrinking. It's what makes IKEA so compelling and Wal-Mart so powerful. Let's look at Wal-Mart's Big Idea, which is "Every item in the store will be offered at the lowest possible price." That's Wal-Mart's reason-for-being and it's an idea that customers and staff alike understand utterly and fundamentally. It is the Big Idea that has driven Sam Walton's company since the moment he articulated it one day when he did a bulk deal on ladies" pants and realized he could be more competitive by passing on the savings to customers.

Don't confuse Big Idea with a marketing strapline: Sometimes they will say broadly the same thing but the idea itself is more than a throwaway

25

creative frippery—it will inform the strapline but will rarely use the exact same words.

Differentiation

Take Wal-Mart's Big Idea and contrast it with Target's, which is to offer "cool things at lower cost." Both sell in roughly the same categories, in the same types of stores (they're classed as "discount variety retailers"). Now, what these two different Big Ideas mean in practice is that Wal-Mart must always opt to sell a 10¢ glass tumbler because it's the cheapest possible price a glass tumbler can be sold for. Target, on the other hand, are able to say "Hmm, that 10¢ tumbler is a bit cheap and nasty. We're about selling at lower cost so we can't stock the really swanky 30¢ tumbler but we've found one that's 12¢ and is a nicer shape, with more consistent molding and heavier glass than Wal-Mart's, so we're going to sell the 12¢ option; it's cheap but it's nice too."

What this has meant is that Target have been able to use their Big Idea to drive a space for themselves to compete against the world's biggest and most powerful retailer. Customers are surprisingly attuned to this sort of subtlety and the result is that Target's customers are younger, wealthier, and better educated than Wal-Mart's.

Let's look at some more Big Ideas in a bit of detail. I'm going to start with more on Wal-Mart because they are so amazingly focused on their Big Idea, and it gives good insight.

Wal-Mart (U.S.)

Every item in the store will be offered at the lowest possible price

Wal-Mart invented the philosophy of "Everyday low pricing" and do more than any other company on earth to drive cost out of their business and to harness the power of bulk purchasing. At one point, Wal-Mart accounted for a staggering 10% of all Chinese exports to the U.S.— buying power demonstrated on a mind-blowing scale. Indeed, Wal-Mart is the biggest company on the planet (by revenue). Because the Big Idea is so clear—in any given product case—Wal-Mart buyers know that they must always choose the option that means they can sell it at the lowest possible cost. Meanwhile every employee understands that cost-reduction is the critical activity—this influences how stores look, where they are and how business is conducted.

Aldi

Simple presentation of an edited supermarket range at the best possible price without compromise on quality

Aldi might be cheap but it isn't nasty and the middle classes across the U.S. and Europe have recognized that quality bargains are a sensible part of the family spend. The stores are plain and very efficient and it costs far less to manage the inventory at Aldi than it does to manage the exponentially larger range at Tesco or Sainsburys. "Edited" is the key word here—Aldi is essentially saying "Trust us, we will stock only the low-cost products that work well, taste nice, or last a long time." This is such a powerfully logical Big Idea that Aldi was able to chase Wal-Mart back out of the German market.

Space.NK (UK)

A carefully edited selection of high-quality, original, and effective beauty products from innovators and specialists around the world

Nicky Kinnaird is an instinctive, natural retailer and Space.NK is brilliant as a result. She recognized that customers want independent advice and recommendations free from single-brand evangelism, that they want help to find the products that do the best job and that are absolutely on-trend. You can't get that at the Clinique or Chanel counters in a department store—you have to do all the work yourself to work out which bits from whose ranges are the best combinations. So Space.NK is almost a living recreation of the "beauty secrets" part of Cosmopolitan or Vogue. It's an incredibly well-focused Big Idea that customers love.

eBay (U.S.)

Connect buyers and sellers, for any product they can imagine, and make that connection easy and safe

It might look like just an auction site, of which a dozen sprouted in the early days of the web, but eBay's success comes from a Big Idea that recognized what buyers and sellers really wanted: to do their buying and selling in the easiest possible way without fear of getting ripped off. It's not really about the mechanics of purchase at all—as the popularity of "Buy it Now" proves. There's a chicken and egg here: eBay's founders understood that they had to attract huge numbers of both buyers and sellers quickly to make other buyers and sellers want to use the site. Again, simplicity and safety were critical—make it easy for people to list their stuff, drop as many barriers to that as possible, and do the same for sellers. Build trust in both and make it scale fast.

MPREIS (Austria)

Local supermarkets built around local produce and each with distinct architectural identity

As well as a focus on local product from the Tyrol region of Austria (each store carries at least 15% Tyrolean products), this one is interesting because the Big Idea affects the very fabric of the stores— each is designed by hot local architects and has a distinctive feel, even though the products inside are consistent between stores. The stores look awesome but it's not design for design's sake: Local customers see their MPREIS as *their* store, not an identikit bland corporate. That's valuable—if a store like MPREIS opened here, you'd shop it.

Apple Store (U.S.)

Taking the Apple brand to the high street in a hands-on and exciting way

Make no mistake, the Apple store is essentially a single-brand PC World, and yet you'd be loath to make the comparison. Apple's Big Idea for their store identity came from outside of electrical retail, from Ron Johnson, former VP of Merchandising at Target. That's crucial to the story because Ron was able to throw away the baggage of electrical retail—hide things away to minimize theft, look but don't touch, cram it in, concentrate only on price—and create a format that reflects Apple's focus on using your technology to do cool stuff. He dovetailed that with lots of support and advice on how to do those things and delivered a format in which the Big Idea means the customer gets to play, become enthused, and be supported in their enthusiasm.

Lush (UK)

A celebration of fresh, natural, and ethically produced body products

Lush are one of the UK's best retail businesses and one of the most genuinely principle-driven—they prove that profit and a conscience are compatible. It's the Big Idea that's interesting here: we're talking vegetarian products, minimal to zero packaging, ethical sourcing standards way above almost anyone else's, public support for controversial direct-action organizations, and an incredible degree of corporate transparency. But do the stores look or feel like campaigning centers for an alternative lifestyle? No, they are a brilliant riot of color, a tidal wave of nice smells, a celebration of great products that work brilliantly and that staff are incredibly proud of. You don't go to Lush hugging a tree and apologizing for wanting to be clean—you go ready to have fun, to be served with passion and laughs, and to come away feeling awesome.

IKEA (Sweden)

Democratizing design: great design, low prices, and accessible to all

Okay, so the flat-pack furniture jokes we used to make about MFI are now directed at IKEA but that's just a by-product of popularity. Actually, what IKEA isn't, and this might be hard to swallow, is a furniture shop—the whole business is built around a set of principles that focus on one thing: making it easy for people to create nice spaces that look good and don't cost too much money. It's a people shop. Building on typically Swedish principles of function before form and simplicity—the store works by first showing customers how to easily group things together, pricing everything in round numbers, filling the journey with fun basics, accessories, and extras to personalize spaces with and then finishing off with an easy collection and payment process all in massive tertiary locations. Yes, it's murder on a weekend but that's because lots of ordinary people like you and me are in there buying cheap things that work well and that look nice doing it. Contrast the experience of buying a first sofa at IKEA now to when you bought your first sofa twenty years ago from a traditional British furniture store … six to eight weeks for delivery, costs a month's wages, probably needed credit to buy it, and it wouldn't have looked much different from your Mom and Dad's. Or your Grandma's. IKEA means everyone can have nice design that functions brilliantly without costing an arm and a leg. That's retail revolution.

Subway (U.S.)

Sandwiches made "fresh" to order

This is an incredibly successful perversion of the idea of fresh food as healthy—Subway invests heavily in promoting the healthy options on its menu, it uses images of crisp hunks of lettuce and juicy fresh tomatoes to lead customers into believing that a sandwich made from scratch in front of them is somehow magically healthier than one wrapped in plastic at the gas station. Every man, woman, and child in the U.S. recognizes Jared, the student who lost half his body weight on a mostly Subway diet for a year. It's so pervasive that people have come to subconsciously see Subway as the healthy fast-food option, even though they actually order meatball marina with extra cheese every time. It's a powerful use of Big Idea but a bit sneaky too.

Costco Wholesale (U.S.)

Limited range in vast depth, serving trade, and employee groups

Easy to see the Big Idea in action here—massive warehouse stocking few lines but each in massive quantity, turning over inventory incredibly fast at low prices. You have to be a "member" to get in and be prepared to buy products in big pack-sizes. For the small-store trade, for offices, hotels, and restaurants, it's another cash and carry but the extension to employee groups is the bit of genius—putting pressure on companies to allow employees access to Costco and giving those employees what feels like a bit of secret access to a part of retail that beats the system.

Media Markt (Germany)

The customer is not stupid and they live where we do

Europe's largest electrical retailer employs a refreshing approach to advertising itself—openly declaring that customers aren't stupid and so should be looked after by knowledgable staff. To deliver great service, Media Markt recognized long ago that store teams who have real say in their store, who get a chance to make decisions, and directly influence outcomes are more likely to want to commit to giving customers great experiences. So stores here are structured as if they were individual businesses—with managers having 10% equity stake and, together with their store team, having a say on assortment, pricing, and advertising based on their local knowledge. People take pride in things they feel ownership of and are able to deliver on Media Markt's Big Idea because of that.

Case study 5.1 Smart Retail: How Hotel Chocolat has helped sideline Thorntons

I like Thorntons. I've got nice memories of buying little bags of Continental truffles as a treat, but the Thorntons I see now ... something is missing. It's lost its way and that's reflected in a decline in trading performance. On ▶

the one hand, Thorntons is actually the UK's largest independent chocolate company; on the other, it's a general confectioner. There's confusion. That confusion follows through to stores where over the door you'll read: "The Art of the Chocolatier." But inside you'll find what appears to be a muddled array of messages and sweets.

And into that confusion, a handful of years ago came the bricks-and-mortar incarnation of catalog chocolate-retailer Hotel Chocolat. And they are wonderful stores pulling off an incredible trick: to be at once cost-effective and mainstream but to appear high-end and authentic. And that's because the business they represent *is* authentic and has set out a Big Idea that defines it as "The Authentic Chocolatier." Now then, that's something everyone can understand and get behind—Hotel Chocolat even own and run a cocoa plantation in St Lucia and aim to not just grow the beans but also to refine the chocolate there. That deep involvement with the fundamental roots of the product shines through to the stores themselves where passion and deep understanding of, and appreciation for, chocolate shines through. You're offered tasty samples by well-presented staff, product is displayed with breathing-space, pride, and care, and lower-priced packs of exciting flavors and combinations of ingredients make the store price-accessible to everyone.

To the customer, Thorntons appear to be about volume and commodity where Hotel Chocolat is about indulgence and authenticity—and is thriving. Thorntons does not have an obvious Big Idea and it's stalling their business. The original Thorntons store was opened in Sheffield in 1911 by Joseph Thornton—when he later handed it over to his two sons, he left them with a Big Idea ringing in their ears "Make this the best sweet shop in town!" And Thorntons *was* that for many of us through the decades, but it isn't *now* and hasn't been for some time. If it was, Thorntons stores would be magical places you'd go to whenever you wanted a special confectionary treat. But they're not—which is sad because there is still room for an evolved Thorntons.

The story of these businesses in a similar market sector shows again how powerful a great Big Idea is.

Case study 5.2 Not Smart Retail: No Big Idea

WHSmith is a fascinating case because the retail company actually consists of two separate businesses: WHSmith High Street and WHSmith Travel, which isn't a travel book shop but rather the WHSmith stores you see at airports, motorway services, and train stations all over the world. One of these doesn't have a Big Idea and one does. One isn't profitable and one is …

WHSmith High Street stocks books, magazines, cards, sweets, stationery, DVDs, CDs and gifts but lead in just one sector—there are better stationers, better book stores, and better music shops; only the magazine section is a leading department. High Street is a business that for more than a decade has had no real idea of what it's actually for. Nobody inside the company actually knows—I've asked.

But WHSmith Travel is brilliant—it's basically the same departments but in highlight form, so you'll have top books with some eclectic promotions, a great range of magazines, batteries, film and camera memory cards, sweets and drinks, and headache tablets—its Big Idea is to reliably equip every traveler with everything they could want to make their journey a better one. The ranges are perfect, the merchandising spot-on, and the checkout-process efficient and pleasant. The Big Idea guides everyone: you know exactly what to look out for as a buyer, exactly what to range as a marketer, and exactly how to present it as a merchandiser. You know because the Big Idea is so clear it drives an obvious and practical mission.

Recently, WHSmith has admitted publicly that High Street is a trading problem while Travel is booming and profitable. Like Thorntons earlier, WHSmith High Street is a business without a Big Idea—they don't know what they're for and neither do customers.

Your Big Idea

What's the Big Idea that drives your retail business? Is it clear? Does it make sense? How does it position you relative to the market and to your competitors? If you're the top person at your place and you answer "no" to any of these questions, please stop reading and go sort it out now. Without that clear understanding of what your business is for, well, there's nothing we can do for you! If you're a team member in-store and you have the misfortune of working for a business that has no Big Idea, see if you can work out what it should be. Make it relevant to your local customers and share it with the team—see if you can use it to at least make *your* store a high-performer. Once you've proved that it has a positive effect, share it with senior management too.

6

CHAPTER SIX

How to build great teams

So, you've got your Big Idea—you know what the business is for and why customers might want a piece of that. Now it's the exciting part—shaping a team that can deliver on that Big Idea. First task is to plan to make that team a happy one ...

Happy teams make you more money. The best customer service is delivered by happy, motivated people. You cannot be a great modern retail business without happy and motivated teams. The best perform-ance improvement strategy I could ever recommend is "make your team happy."

A happy team of friendly motivated people, pulling together, having fun with customers, bristling with ideas and enthusiasm, people with passion for the job, can build huge performance improvements. Like so much in retail, the recommendation to create a happy team is very, very obvious, but is also a massive challenge. The best of us still struggle to get every new hire right, to always make the best decision in a given situation, to not drop the ball when the going gets tough. Management is hard to do right—that is why business rates good managers so highly.

Because managing people is hard, great teams are still the exceptions rather than the rule. That's actually a good thing for you. Think of it as competitive advantage through team building.

A consistency I've seen through great retail businesses is that they under-stand their Big Idea, tend to be very clear on what the business is trying to do (mission), allow people to behave like grown-ups (respect) and are very good at recognizing positive behaviors (recognition). Let's call these three things "cornerstones": Mission, Respect, Recognition. Wherever the three are in evidence, great team and store cultures emerge and I firmly believe that this is a bit of a secret, if there is such a thing, of great leadership:

Cornerstone 1   Mission: We understand what we want to do for our customers.

Cornerstone 2   Respect: We make sure our people know they are empowered to do those things.

Cornerstone 3   Recognition: We reinforce those positive things by recognizing them when they happen.

The three then exist as a self-reinforcing loop: the clearer we are about what our business is for and the better we enable our people to do those things, and the more we notice and say "thank you" when they do them, then the better we become.

I'll go into each cornerstone in more detail over the next few pages but first I want to illustrate the value and importance of a great store culture. I would also like to show you that your individual store culture can still be a great one even if the wider company culture isn't.

Leadership

Things get a little bit tricky when we start to think about leadership and teams. I have a heartfelt belief that leadership cannot be taught—indeed we once lost out on a large bit of consultancy business because I fundamentally disagreed with the notion that leadership could be taught: A UK retailer with 1300 stores was looking to improve store cultures and was very proud of the expensive leadership program they had pushed 1300 managers through. But when we peeled back the detail of what had actually happened, it became clear that any gains they'd seen as a result of this leadership program were pretty much down to the fact that those 1300 managers had spent two days out of their stores and were hyper-aware that senior people were watching them like hawks post-course. It was also clear that those gains would evaporate quite quickly. And here's where we lost the relationship: I'm not sure that the role of Human Resources is to teach a fundamental in-the-genes skill such as leadership. No, I believe its job is to find the best existing 1300 leaders out there within the total 48,000-strong workforce and then to put those natural leaders in the right roles. Pointing that out led to a huge disconnect from that particular client and we've not been back since. When I say "disconnect" I do, of course, mean "hissy fit"; as expected, their leadership program didn't work and this company has experienced flat or declining performance in the seven years since I first wrote about them. I don't want to be crowing "I told you so"—that doesn't generate invoices—but, well, "I told you so."

So, do you have to be a good leader to be a great retailer? Do you have to be a good leader to create a strong store culture? The painful answer is that to a large degree, yes, you do. You might want to do a bit of soul-searching for a moment on that. It might help if I define leadership—it's really about answering one question: Are you able to inspire others to line up behind your chosen course of action?

Now—having got you through that (I'm hoping you answered "yes"), we get to the notion that great leaders can, and sometimes do, still fall on their behinds. Being able to lead is essential to the job at hand, but understanding where to lead and how to structure the journey is essential too. And that's where your Mission–Respect–Recognition cornerstones come in handy; it's like a leadership map: Follow those steps and you'll get to where you want to go.

Let's look at why it's worth making a great store culture one of your destinations.

Why bother building a great team?

Improved customer service

Customers prefer to be served by happy friendly people—every observational study proves that conclusively. Tied in to improvements in employee retention (see p. 38) are corresponding improvements in employee effectiveness and knowledge. People who stay with you longer tend to get better at their jobs and that filters through directly to the customer experience.

> **Customers prefer to be served by happy friendly people—every observational study proves that conclusively.**

▶ Customers come back more often and they rave about you.

▶ Customers return to stores that feel good to be in—the "people" part of a store is critical to that feeling.

▶ Customers share their great experiences, most of which relate to how your people have looked after them.

Cost savings

▶ Reduced shrinkage—happy people don't steal from you and they care more about reducing customer theft as well

▶ Reduced employee turnover—happy people, and people who feel valued, stay with you longer and that means savings not only on advertising for replacements but also savings on training and your time.

Walking the talk

We cover values and mission statements later (don't yawn, we're talking practical advice, not management consultant waffle), when I'll explain why these are so important to the success of your business. A great store culture makes an excellent starting point for making values and mission statements really work for you. Walking the talk also means that new ideas tend to be adopted more readily and more happily by the team: Everybody is up for driving the team forwards.

Support

You could create a happy team by letting everyone run riot, throw parties whenever they want, and help themselves to whatever they fancy from the stockroom. That of course wouldn't do anything for the performance of the business. A great store culture still encompasses the unpleasant things such as firing people who don't make the grade and reprimanding staff when they let the team down. However, if you have that great culture built and you have a happy team, they will tend to be far more supportive of you in those difficult decisions. That's useful because it helps keep the disruption of such moments down to a minimum and the team gets over it more quickly.

Enjoyment

Fun is a powerful component in a high-performing team. Happy teams are nicer to work within. Fun is a powerful component in a high-performing team. Shopping is in itself fun: In all but a few circumstances, customers like getting to go out and buy stuff so it's reasonable to aim for a fun store culture too.

Reasons not to?

A lot of managers say "the company culture is so awful that I can't make a difference here in my store." Although I'm sympathetic to the additional pressure a bad company culture puts on its store managers, I can't accept this as a real excuse to avoid building a great store culture. Retail superstar Julian Richer has this to say about the ability of a store manager to lead culture in their own store: "The culture of the store is determined by the manager and then we try to get our company culture on top of that." It's managers who create the store culture, not head office.

Why assistant managers must become "keepers" of the culture

Richer also remarked that "it is sad whenever a store manager leaves." It is indeed sad when a great store manager leaves, and it can often mean the death of a team. This is why store managers should work closely with their assistant managers in planning and building a great culture. Aim to leave a little bit of yourself behind so that whoever takes over, ideally your assistant store manager, can strengthen the culture further, building on your work. For most of us, and I include myself in this, there is massive pleasure to be had from discovering that something you helped build is still solid and in play years later.

Service Profit Chain

I'm not keen on theory for its own sake and I get irritated by diagrams that have more to do with consultants trying to be clever than making a clear point, and that's why there's just the one diagram in the whole of this book. It's a pretty important one though—some years ago, I was introduced to the basic idea that within retail and service organizations, it's employees who have the biggest impact on customers" experience of the brand. Sounds obvious when you put it like that, and it's true. What Service Profit Chain theory does is turn the fluffy bit of that equation into a way to measure the pound-note impact of treating your employees with respect, care, and integrity.

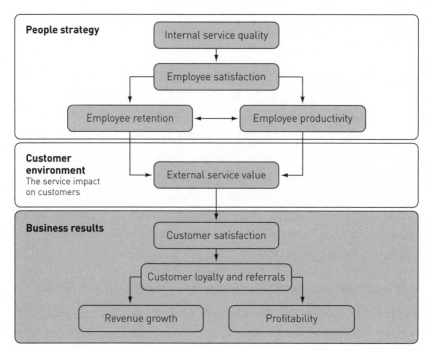

People strategy

Internal service quality

Employee satisfaction

Employee retention ⟷ Employee productivity

Customer environment
The service impact on customers

External service value

Business results

Customer satisfaction

Customer loyalty and referrals

Revenue growth

Profitability

"Nice" means profit.
Source: Smart Circle Limited

Let's step through those boxes then:

Internal service quality

▶ Treating your people well is good.

Employee satisfaction

▶ Because happy, motivated, and respected staff are more satisfied.

Employee retention

▶ They stay longer with you.

Employee productivity

▶ They get better at their jobs.

External service value

▶ And happy, stable, and productive teams tend to deliver the best customer service experiences.

Customer satisfaction

▶ Which makes customers happy.

Customer loyalty and referrals

▶ And they come back more often, spend more money with you, and they recommend you to their pals.

Revenue growth

▶ Which means you stuff your registers with wads of cash.

Profitability

▶ Goes up and up and we all start to have baths filled with money instead of water.

And the thing is, the logic of this process is inescapable and can be seen at work inside the world's best retailers—yet it's rarer than it should be. Putting Misson, Respect, and Recognition at the heart of your management style will deliver this good stuff. Great employment experiences drive great customer experiences and that probably equals promotions all around.

The three cornerstones

Let's just recap on those three cornerstones I mentioned earlier:

Cornerstone 1: Mission
We understand what we want to do for our customers.

Cornerstone 2: Respect
We make sure our people know they are empowered to do those things.

Cornerstone 3: Recognition
We reinforce those positive things by recognizing them when they happen.

So now on to the detail!

Cornerstone 1   The Mission

Practical people slaving away at the worksite have a rational dislike of mission statements. We tend to think of them as nothing more than marketing waffle. I suspect that is because we have been subjected to so many awful mission statements that just didn't mean anything. That's a shame because a good mission statement is an incredibly powerful tool. It becomes a rallying point for the whole team.

Has your company got a mission statement? If it has, does it make sense? Does it make clear what it is that the business wants you to do? Does it help you to make choices and decisions? Above all does it reflect the Big Idea (for really good ones, they are exactly the same—same words, same meaning)? If the answer to those questions is "no" then you are going to need to re-write the mission statement yourself. Once you have done that, you must make that statement live and breathe; refer to it in every team meeting and offer up every decision and choice you make against it.

A strong, clear mission statement can be a fantastic tool for improving and securing best performance. Make it simple, obvious, reinforcing, and make sure too that it addresses practical objectives.

Case study 6.1 Smart Retail: Best Buy some trust

Best Buy has a powerful mission statement—indeed, it's so strong they don't even bother to call it a mission statement. It's just something bred so deeply into the company that it's become a natural reflex answer to the question "How come you're so successful then, Mr Best Buy?"

Our formula is simple: We're a growth company focused on better solving the unmet needs of our customers—and we rely on our employees to solve those puzzles. Thanks for stopping by.

You work for Best Buy in one of its stores? You know that mission statement means the company wants you to actually talk to customers and find out what they really need and want and then do your best to match those needs and wants with the right product. To help you do that, Best Buy put you through an unprecedented nine-week training and induction program before you get anywhere near a customer. More than sales-staff though—it's a mission that tells you how to merchandise a store, what products to look out for as a buyer, and how to present them. It's a mission that helped shape remuneration packages (no commission), training (making training central to delivering the Big Idea), and recruitment (hiring people good at listening as well as talking—not sales jocks). These are things that aren't common currency in electrical retail and that's why customers love Best Buy.

Fits really well with the Big Idea at Best Buy too—which is to create massive electrical retail stores in which staff can be trusted to be as honest, relevant, helpful, and accurate as staff in a small independent.

Values

This is another area where a lot of awful trash has been spouted by management gurus. It means that talking about values can feel a little ridiculous. This is a shame because a set of defined values becomes the practical tool that helps you to apply the mission statement to the everyday running of the store. Where the mission statement tells you what the company does, the values tell you how it wants to go about doing it. They are a reflection of what the company stands for. We're talking about a list of words such as innovative, fun, honest, and inspirational. The trick is to mold these values into a set of practical sentences that tell us how to apply the values to the jobs we do every day.

A great way to think about values is to fix in your mind the perfect customer experience in your store, then imagine talking to that customer outside afterwards; what five emotions might they tell you they felt during that experience? Write down that list of emotions and then ask yourself this question: If my customers leave my store feeling those five things—are they likely to come back again? If the answer is "yes" then you're on to something good.

Walking the talk

Defining a good mission statement and then living the values in-store—"walking the talk"—is good for you because it improves the customer experience and builds stronger teams; this in turn increases business performance. In a case such as the Best Buy one, walking the talk in store

Big Idea and mission perfectly expressed right there.
Source: Koworld

is doubly powerful because everything the central team does, such as advertising, promotions, and store investment, is also right in line with the mission and values. They strengthen each other.

If you work in a business that has a clear and consistent set of values, use them to your advantage. Live and breathe them: "walk the talk" will improve performance. In an independent store, you too must define a mission and a set of values—everything else flows from them.

A good set of mission and values reads naturally: It uses language that a normal person can easily make sense of. Simple things—strongly stated.

Case study 6.2 Smart Retail: Values in action at a leading fashion store

Here is a solid practical example of the way in which values can make a significant difference to the everyday functioning of your shop. This case study is about a British clothes retailer. One of the very obvious values that applied to this business was that buying or selling clothes was about fun: It's a fun thing to do. Customers wanted a happy environment and staff wanted to enjoy their jobs. In fact, that was one of the things people told us had attracted them to the business; working in fashion retail looked like it might be more fun than stacking shelves. So we included fun as a value. It really supported the company mission too. That mission statement read "To delight our customers by giving them affordable access to great high street fashion."

Fun is a value that many people believe, and I agree, should be part of the working environment for almost any retailer. I don't mean mindless larking about but the generation of genuine "this is cool" moments for customers and staff alike. Fun helps make shopping enjoyable. We are all in the business of making shopping fun, whether we are selling washing machines or watches.

Fun with job descriptions

One of my favorite methods for making values work every day in-store is to rewrite job descriptions. Out goes the dry HR-speak and in comes practical stuff about what to do and why. In the case of this retailer, we had identified one particular group of employees who were really hard to engage. There was a set of 16–18-year-old girls who all worked one weekday evening and then all day Saturday. They are notoriously hard to engage. You hardly see them all week and then suddenly they are there on your busiest day when you've got little time to give them. It's crucial that you have these girls on board and pulling for the team or they can become a disruptive and negative element in the store. They are also famous for degrees of lateness and for being uncommitted when they do finally arrive. This was especially true on hung-over Saturday mornings!

We looked at their job descriptions which, and to be honest I can't blame them, I doubt any of the girls themselves had read. One of the most important responsibilities, in fact the first task they were supposed to perform on Saturday mornings, read like this: "You will ensure all merchandise rails, shelves, and/or islands are fully filled and merchandised in accordance with the prevailing marketing planogram for your store grade and profile." Of course what this actually meant was simply "Make sure there are no gaps on display when we let the shoppers in." The girls ▶

45

regarded this responsibility as a real chore: boring. Not the sort of thing they wanted to do when arriving tired after a big Friday night out.

So we changed it—we introduced that value of fun. The same line from the job description now read: "Fashion is fun, remember that as you dive into the stockroom and pull out your favorite, most exciting fashions. We want you to take your choices, the clothes you think customers should be wearing out tonight, onto the sales-floor. Get them onto the racks, anywhere there are gaps, and get your choices noticed." When we tested it, the effect was fantastic.

Because we had asked the girls to think for themselves—and who really is best placed to say what the trendiest clothes for 16–18-year-old girls are than a group of 16–18-year-old girls—they actually got excited by the task, even beginning to come in early to get the best picks. They also got competitive with each other and would jostle for space and monitor each other's selections like hawks. Very healthy stuff indeed with the unexpected side effect that the girls also began to sell proactively. They would make sure every customer saw their personal picks and they would ensure a constant supply of sizes and colors was always out on display. That's how a mission statement and a clear set of values can have a direct effect on the performance of the team.

Street Time

Now that you've read about Big Ideas, Mission, and Values—please have a look at the Street Time tool in Appendix III. As well as being good fun to do, it's something that will help you to go out and find many ways to improve and change your businesses.

Cornerstone 2 | Respect

Treat people how you yourself would wish to be treated. My Grandma used to say that to me—and like a lot of the wisdom of her generation, it's absolutely on the money. In today's retail landscape, you have no option but to treat your people with respect. Here's why ...

A disrespectful market

The mobile-phone retail business enjoyed, or suffered, a yo-yo sales curve during the 1990s and into the 2000s. Excellent businesses such as Carphone Warehouse (CPW) were not immune when the market first dipped sharply. But when picture messaging and color-screen phones (wow, sounds like the sort of phone my Grandad would have used) helped re-ignite the market, CPW benefited more than most. Carphone Warehouse is the honest phone retailer that emerged out of a time when the sector was dominated by sharks and cowboys. This is a retailer that prides itself on looking after everybody's needs: customers and staff alike. It is a retailer whose successful employment policy is built on respect. It is also a retailer that has benefited from the very positive knock-on effects of such a policy.

Talk to an employee of CPW and they will tell you that the work is hard, the hours long, and the standards are stretching and rigorously applied. They will also tell you that they enjoy it enormously. Push a little harder: ask them "Why do you enjoy it here?" A consistent story emerges:

- ▶ "We get treated with respect."
- ▶ "I'm trained so well that I never look stupid in front of customers."
- ▶ "My ideas are worth something."
- ▶ "I'm allowed, no I'm encouraged, to use my brain."
- ▶ "It's made clear that I can have a proper career at Carphone Warehouse if I want one."

So, now how are things for CPW? The company thrived, has pushed through another recession, and continues to lead with its principles of respect, fairness, and honesty intact. It's no coincidence that they have also aligned themselves closely with another leader that is built on similar principles—CPW and Best Buy now have a number of joint ventures, including 50/50 ownership of Carphone Warehouse and Best Buy stores in Europe. Respect and honesty, it seems, pays.

An alternative approach can be seen in the same marketplace. Back in 2003, Phones 4u was featured in a fascinating TV documentary. In one now infamous scene, a manager was shown enjoying the dubious honor of receiving what could be considered as quietly threatening phone calls from the then millionaire chairman John Caudwell. These phone calls were to remind that manager that he had but one week to improve the numbers or face the sack. That's a classic example of management by fear rather than management by respect. I asked Phones 4u at the time how they felt about the picture portrayed in that documentary. They told me the result had been an upsurge in job applications from people they called "real go-getters, the sort of people who respond to a bit of pressure."

When I wrote the first edition of *Smart Retail*, I said I was keen to see how this attitude would pan out for customers over the long term. The short answer is that Carphone Warehouse ran away with the prize, John Caudwell sold Phones 4u (for a tidy profit, mind) and the business has spent the last seven years working hard to improve its customer service standards as well as improving the way it manages its people. And guess what—it's working but perhaps too slowly to significantly dent Carphone Warehouse's lead. Customers have long memories ...

Flight to quality

In a fast-growing market, where price and availability are the overriding considerations, many customers will happily buy from the cheapest outfit regardless of reputation. The situation then changes quickly when market conditions tighten and saturation is reached. In the slowdown, customers gravitate to quality, they think a little more carefully about what they want, and they look for reliable sources of good advice. Then, when things begin to pick up again, customers often stick with the new relationships they've formed. They value those relationships with retailers who have looked after them knowledgeably, honestly, and with a smile. More than that—in an era in which customers have lots of choice, they tend to vote with their feet and go where the best overall experiences are. Technically it's called a "flight to quality"—which is jargon, but it's jargon that makes sense.

We saw this in 2010 as the UK ground out of recession—sales at Waitrose, of Tesco's "Finest" range, of premium brands such as Sony and L'Oréal all grew where lower mid-range brands saw shrinkage. Right now, being a retailer who has proven to be a provider of great customer experiences is showing real sales benefits: Customers get fed up with austerity shopping and, while still spending less overall, they start to put what they do spend into nice purchases: "We'll have nice week at the seaside this year but then a big family adventure to the Caribbean next year—instead of our usual annual trips to Spain."

The 1980s retail legacy

Back in the 1980s, there was a surge in consumer-spending. In the UK, this surge ran alongside unprecedented levels of unemployment—for some everything was rosy and for others desperate. A group of UK retailers became incredibly successful off the back of the surge but some chose to exploit their workforces, knowing that the threat of unemployment loomed large. With demand for fashion, food, and consumer goods out-stripping supply at times, leading stores were able to sell almost everything they could present. The best of these looked after their staff well and saw background unemployment as a reason to be a good employer rather than a bad one. On the flip side were those retailers who saw people as dispos-able, an expendable resource to be bullied into line. Customers were blind to the effects of this as they scrambled over themselves to buy, buy, buy and so the bully-boy retailers got away with treating staff badly.

I started in-store in 1985 and witnessed the worst of this first-hand: a man-agement style emerged, and it was called JFDI, or "just flipping do it" (you and I both know that I've changed one of those words to a print-friendly alternative). JFDI was anti-respect: It was all about conformity and sub-servience. I first entered retailing in the middle of these years and it was mean at times. Nasty even. It was an atmosphere that chewed people up, burnt them out, took advantage of job insecurity, and made some people's lives a horrid experience.

But come the early 1990s and the boom and bust cycle was beginning to flatten; with that flattening came a calming in the rabid consumerism and large reductions in levels of unemployment—a longer-term sustain-able prosperity was established. And something happened in the way people, especially in the UK, shopped: They became more discerning, as if the hangover of the 1980s was accompanied by an understanding that spending for the sake of spending wasn't a great idea any more.

And customers appeared to begin to notice that those businesses run on the principles of JFDI weren't nice places to shop. Customers aren't stupid: They might not be able to define what it is that they notice in a JFDI-led store, but it does affect them.

This effect is just one very good reason to invest in and show respect for your staff. Forget even the straightforward cost benefits of keeping your staff longer; the simple reality is that teams built on respect and passion ultimately bring more profit into your business. Teams built on fear and unreasonable pressure do often create short-term sales gains but they always crack, and usually this happens very quickly. What is more, they leave customers feeling negative about their interaction with the brand and less inclined to ever come back again. In an age of real-time access to live sales numbers, it can be easy to fall back, under pressure, into a JFDI management style. Don't. What your business gains today it will lose tomorrow and next week.

Teams built on respect and passion ultimately bring more profit into your business.

The respect deal

Respect, thankfully, is a two-way street. Yes, you will still have to deal with under-performing colleagues. Yes, you might find yourself having to exit people from your business. That is always hard to do but in a team that has been built on respect, you will have worked hard with that person to make things right. The people in your team will know that and will support your decisions rather than becoming unsettled by them.

We have that phrase "You have to earn respect"; well, in retail management that gets warped a little. You, as a manager, have to earn respect from your team, sure—but you must respect them from day one! People are always wary of change, which is why you will have to work hard to earn their respect. But this is not a mutual deal. Even before you first meet your team you have to respect them. If you didn't, if you came into a new store with an attitude that said "I'm in charge and until I know you I am reserving my judgement," then people tend to turn off.

Luckily, the most effective way to earn respect is to give it! If you systematically go about building trust, recognizing people's contribution, sharing training and creating opportunities for personal growth, then you will build a strong successful team that likes and respects you. You will have gone a long way to building a brilliant culture.

For some great tips on how to build respect, read Chapter 5 which is on Motivation; I've listed a whole series of them there.

Case study 6.3 Smart Retail: Top Shop instinct, respect, and risk

> I have this thing about men in suits, you know. People who drone on about the principles of retail. What bollocks! There aren't any principles of retailing.[1]
>
> Jane Shepherdson—former brand director, Top Shop.[2]

Top Shop is the British retailer born as a concession in a Sheffield department store in 1964. Gloriously it has never held itself to be anything more than a store selling cheap and cheerful clothes to young women. Shepherdson took on the top job in 1999—Top Shop's thirty-fifth year—and transformed it utterly, not in terms of market position, or, necessarily, the type of clothes it sells but by making the store exciting, unpredictable, passionate, and anti-marketing. By that I mean that she has drilled into her entire team that they must ignore the rules and do what feels natural instead. This was, at the time, a huge risk—a proper gamble.

Top Shop's Big Idea is brilliantly simple: Be our own customers, forget the needs of the business. That's shocking but it's an attitude, a revolution indeed, that has put Top Shop among the world's most high-profile and successful retailers.

Here's an example of how Jane forced the rules to be broken by thinking like a customer: "I would go into meetings and say 'Yes, I know that's selling and it's selling two thousand units but I don't care, it's awful and we're not going to buy awful things any more regardless of whether or not they will sell.' If you're going to earn people's trust, you have to set a standard. That set the standard—all the buyers now know that, and all the buyers now stand by every single thing in their range. Compare this to ten or twenty years ago when some buyers would sit there saying, 'have you ▶

seen this, isn't it horrible? Guess how many we sold last week ... isn't that great?' I thought it was outrageous. How could they do that? It's not right, there's no integrity."

How often have you dropped a profitable product because you don't think your customers should be buying it? "Never" is the answer for most of us. What that kind of thinking has done at Top Shop, together it has to be said with modern just-in-time logistics allowing fast stock turn, is to create a store that feels utterly in tune with customers. It's risk that is at the heart of that transformation.

The power of standing for something, of building the retail business around that Big Idea, then living and breathing it, is the best-kept secret in retailing. It's a passionate, instinctive thing and at the heart of every successful retail business.

[1]   The Jane Shepherdson quotes in this case study are based on an interview contained within Martin Butler's essential book on retailing, *People Don't Buy What You Sell (They Buy What You Stand For)*.

[2]   Although Jane moved on from Top Shop in 2006, there is absolutely no doubt that the incredible continued success there is directly attributable to her revolution, attitude, and love of fashion-risk.

Ownership—the value of mistakes

Mistakes are great. Mistakes are brilliant—get on with making things happen, make mistakes and learn from them, and try more stuff.

People make mistakes when you let them make decisions. They get a lot right too. Being as close as they are to where the action is, your team is absolutely the best people to be making more decisions for the business.

And yet, providing local decision-making tools to individual stores is something that fills most retail directors with horror. It is easy to see how senior central management can get scared about letting their store managers loose. But all the evidence tells us that this is wrong. Wherever proper decision-making power has been delegated down to individual store teams, it has led to increased sales and profit. Yes, it has also, sometimes, resulted in more mistakes being made. But mistakes are only unlearned lessons. You make one, you learn from it, and you move on.

Maybe that sounds a little too much like a homespun philosophy but it also happens to be true. Think about the early careers of people like Richard Branson, bankrupt in his teens, or Ray Kroc, the genius behind McDonald's, who had a string of mistakes, false starts, and lean times behind him when, at 62, he spotted the potential for franchised fast-food. Mistakes are made when you try something new, different, or difficult. Sure, you reduce your errors down to zero if you never try anything, but just see what happens to your business when you do that.

Cornerstone 3   Recognition

Recognition is the bit that happens when you are saying "thank you" to somebody you've caught doing good things. It is the single most powerful motivation tool in life, let alone in business. Teams used to receiving recognition give better customer service, work happier together, are more efficient, are more stable, and they make life at work more enjoyable for all. That is because when you recognize an employee's contribution you send out a very strong message that says "I'm glad you came to work today, you made a difference." There's more to motivation than just recognition but it is recognition that is most important—we'll deal with the other parts in the next chapter.

Most people want to do the best job they can in any given situation; recognition is the tool that tells them it has been worth making the effort. Recognition is self-reinforcing: People want to do a good job, you recognize them for it when they do, they feel good, so they repeat the recognized action because they like feeling good. Maybe this is a simplified representation of what actually goes on in our heads, but do you see how small moments of praise can escalate into improved performance?

Given that recognition is so powerful, why is it that retail managers are almost never trained in or assessed on their ability to effectively recognize? I believe there are some simple reasons, mostly relating to how hard it is to both measure recognition and to definitively define a list of exact things that should be recognized: They might include such things as improving team spirit, giving exceptional customer service, or going the extra mile. Recognition is less about direct sales numbers, although you will want to recognize contribution in that area too.

I suspect that it's the free nature of recognition that puts number-obsessed chain retailers off using it. This is a trust issue, head office not being prepared to trust that it is managers in the store, on the spot, who have the best view of the people around them. Recognition is free—it doesn't cost a penny and can drive store performance more effectively than almost any other management tool I have ever seen. You simply must use it.

Please don't make a fuss

One of the issues that makes recognition hard to do at first is a cultural one. The British are embarrassed by praise, we struggle to accept it. Indeed the most common response among British workers to receiving praise is to blush and to break eye contact. The strange parallel to that praise response is that we generally do not have the same problem when receiving criticism. When on the receiving end of criticism, most British workers will listen, if not always graciously, but they will listen. We all tend to have a system for receiving criticism, maybe not always a positive system but it is nonetheless a system. When it comes to receiving praise, although we really like the feeling, we are a little unsure of how to react.

There is also a crucial difference between the delivery of praise and of criticism. We tend to be specific when criticizing but only general when praising. It is this lack of clarity, I believe, that makes people so bad at giving and receiving praise. We give usefully specific criticism such as "the budget you did isn't right, where are the print costs?" whereas praise would be vague, "nice work on the budget." This is important because the whole point of praise and recognition is that we do it in such a way that recipients understand exactly what they did well so that they can repeat that behavior. In the budget example above, the person who has been criticized knows they have to now go and sort out the print costs. The other person, praised with the "nice work on the budget" comment has no idea why this budget was better than the last one, or what it was exactly that they ought to repeat to get some more praise next time. Better praise would have been "I like how you've laid out the budget. That's going to make it easier for me to get it approved. Thanks."

"Doing" recognition

"Little and often" is a brilliant management maxim. It's absolutely perfect when applied to recognition. To make too much of a moment of praise can make everybody feel uncomfortable. It can even sometimes encourage resentment from the team toward whoever you have singled out for extra-double helpings of praise. You are not attempting to make an individual feel like they are God's gift to retail. If the thing they've done is really special then by all means mention it at a team meeting. But for the rest of the time, the best way to "do" recognition is this: spot something good, mention it quickly, say "thank you," and be specific.

The bad recognition-habits we managers get into, often because we're embarrassed by praise, include: worrying about singling out individuals, delaying praise, over-blowing praise, concentrating on catching people getting it wrong, and the inability to be specific with our praise. Delaying praise reduces the effectiveness of recognition. Recognition works best when fresh.

Too many people build their management style around spotting staff making mistakes and then correcting the errors. If you are one of them, try catching people doing good things instead. Do that and you will quickly find that staff actively attempt to repeat those good things and that they look for more and more good things to do. Recognition taps into so many crucial psychological needs. The easy bit to accept is that recognition, done properly, makes people feel good.

> **Recognition taps into so many crucial psychological needs.**

It is nice also to link recognition to small rewards, but this isn't at all critical. Study after study shows that the part employees actually value is that moment where their manager, or a colleague, or a customer, says "thank you for ..."

Behaviors

Although a good recognition habit is all about being spontaneous, saying "thank you" whenever you see the need, it helps to have in mind a list of the sorts of things that you will be looking out to give praise for. At the risk of sounding like I've been snacking on a jargon cookie, what you should be basing your recognition on are "observable positive behaviors." Essentially that's all the good stuff people do that you can spot them doing.

When you first decide to introduce recognition, putting together a list of these "observable positive behaviors" helps the whole team to get a handle on what it is that you are looking for. Once you've sat down and really thought about these behaviors, you can stick a list up on the noticeboard. Give a copy to new starters, and use it as a basis for review meetings.

"Observable" is the key word in this bit of jargon. It tells you that the behaviors you are looking for are those that you actually have to "see" happen. Sales is not an "observable positive behavior" because it is an activity that (a) you already measure closely in the performance numbers, and (b) you will be discussing the sales action with each member of the team anyway. How a person makes a sale though—that could easily include a positive observable behavior: going out of their way to find a bit of information for a customer, or selling an item that was right for the customer but that had a lower commission-rate on it for the salesperson.

Those "observable positive behaviors" that relate to helping make customers happy are important. With any luck, such behavior will show up as a sale, but even if it doesn't, that customer has left the store with a good feeling about your business. That is worth its weight in gold but in a way that is very hard to see from looking just at the hard performance numbers.

Take a look at the "Great moments" section in Chapter 9 for a little set of illustrations of observable positive behaviors in action.

Easy ways to "do" recognition

There are two easy routes you can go down to build recognition into your team culture. Doing specific recognition needs to be learned, so don't be embarrassed that it might not be part of your current style. You will get there by practice. Equally, don't assume that because you do often say "thank you" that you are getting recognition right. I'll lay down good money that, when you are honest with yourself, you will find that 90% of those "thank you" moments are non-specific.

In the years between the first edition and the one you're reading now, loads of managers have fed back that this part of the book is the one they were most skeptical about but that once done had been the most rewarding. I guess I'm saying "disconnect the cynicism for a bit and give this stuff a go—you'll be glad you did."

Method one—The 20-second ceremony

Use a couple of team meetings to make up your team's list of "observable positive behaviors." A good way to get a great list together is to start with the Big Idea, the mission, and values too, and think about the kind of things you can do to support them.

Now make up some "thank you" notes. These should have space on for the recipient's name and a bigger space for you to write down why you are pleased enough to want to say "thank you." Print out a bunch of these and keep some in your pocket at all times. Whenever you see an opportunity to say "thank you," fill one out quickly and go put it into the hand of the person you want to say "thanks" to. You don't even have to say "thanks" if you don't feel you can. You don't have to make a song and dance of it, you don't even have to speak if you feel uncomfortable. What is important is that the exchange of this note is something both of you understand: It tells the recipient that you have noticed and that you are pleased, nothing more, nothing less. Takes about 20 seconds to do.

Dish out blank "thank you" notes to the team as well. Encourage everyone to use these "thank you" notes. Workmates recognizing each other's efforts has almost as much power as when you do it. You have really cracked it when you get customers to fill in "thank you" notes.

The 20-second ceremony works so well and is unobtrusive: I've seen this work successfully in a tiny KFC that was processing 50,000 lunch transactions a week. People really do respond to it. The notes can feel a bit silly at first but that soon goes and the process of recognition becomes part of the everyday team culture. You will never find a cheaper or more effective way in which to transform your team's performance.

Method two—The Heroes Board

Allocate a piece of wall space to recognition. Make up some "thank-you" notes similar to the ones mentioned above. Start giving them to people under the same criteria, and tell recipients to hang them up on the wall. This method introduces a little bit of peer pressure because everyone can see who is being praised, but you might find it more comfortable for you than recognition method one.

In both methods, you can use the best examples to determine what you do with your non-cash rewards (which we go through in Chapter 5). It's quite nice to build in a little focus at team meetings for recognition. It's even more effective to use one such meeting, each week, for a little bit of extra recognition. Take the best "thank you" or "hero" example from that week and give the person a decent bottle of wine, a case of beer, flowers, or good chocolates. Not too much, but it feels great to receive, and it really sets the scene for a rousing and effective team meeting.

Case study 6.4 Smart Retail: KFC and the 20-second recognition ceremony

KFC transformed their business in the UK in the late 1990s and have strengthened their position ever since. It is a fantastic retail business. One of the major transformation focuses was on the way in which they treated their people. As part of that process, they introduced a recognition program based on observable positive behaviors and on the 20-second recognition ceremony.

A beautiful example of how this tiny, simple, ceremony could affect the way people felt about themselves and their performance came to me at a post-launch regional meeting. A manager, Mike, told me what had happened when he went through the 20-second ceremony for the first time. In fact he told me he'd made somebody cry doing it, so I thought we might be in trouble. Dawn had worked at her KFC outlet for nearly 10 years. She had seen managers come and go but had never been keen to take on that sort of extra responsibility for herself. She liked being one of the team and that was that. Mike had been her manager for nearly six months.

One morning Mike spotted Dawn showing a new member of staff how to "double-bag" a waste bin. Double-bagging means putting in two bin-liners at a time so that at lunch, when the bin is full, you only have to throw one bag of waste away and the bin already has its next liner in place. Now this is a tiny thing, saves maybe a minute at peak time. But Mike saw Dawn do this and it occurred to him that he had seen Dawn help new people learn the ropes on countless occasions. She didn't have to, it wasn't part of her job, she just liked to do it. So Mike decided to use one of his "thank you" notes. He wrote it out and ticked a box that said "For making new members of the team feel welcome" and, in his own words he "shyly handed it to Dawn."

Dawn burst into tears. Mike reassured her that it wasn't a P45 he'd just given her and asked what the matter was. So she told him "You've never said 'thank you' to me before." Mike became quite indignant and replied that he had, often, at shift meetings. Dawn put him right. "No, you've said 'thanks' to the team, and that's nice but you've never come to me, looked me in the eye, and made it so clear that something good I do has been noticed. And actually none of my managers over the years has either."

Dawn felt great about that moment of recognition—that's why there were tears. Most people feel the same way. What's so nice about this approach is that its effect snowballs. Slowly but surely, more people begin to repeat the good things they do more often, and that gently spreads throughout the business.

Why recognition works

Why does specific recognition like that work so powerfully? It's about clarity: You say to somebody "Well done, good job today" and it feels good to that person for a bit, but when they later ask themselves "What did I do different that meant I got praise today?" it's difficult to actually know for sure. When instead you say "Well done, thanks—you've made that new person feel welcome and I appreciate it, helps to bring us closer as a team" that staff member walks away knowing exactly what behaviors to repeat in order to get nice praise again.

7

CHAPTER SEVEN

How to get people out of bed

Motivated staff are critical to the success of your store. Hopefully you will have already read the previous chapter on store cultures (the mission and values stuff). If you have, then you are already on the way to enjoying the benefits of having a motivated team around you. In this section, we're going to get a bit deeper into the nitty gritty of motivation. In particular, I'd like to suggest some practical moves you can make to improve the motivation of your team.

If you're going to build a great culture in your store, a motivated team is essential. Just to recap, the benefits of a great store culture include cost savings, customer service quality improvements, people pulling together to deliver the company values, better support for your decisions, and a more enjoyable time at work.

The components of motivation

Individuals are motivated by a combination of:

▶ **Financial reward**

▶ **Implied sanction**

▶ **Self-respect**

▶ **Non-financial reward**

▶ **Recognition of value contributed**

Of course, the importance of each motivating component will be different for different people. Factors such as age, personal circumstances, and social considerations all have an impact. Most of these, with one exception, make for only really subtle changes in your approach. The younger members of your team are often disproportionately motivated by cash. You might think "well, isn't everyone"—over the next few pages, I'll show you why that's not quite true.

Show me the money—financial reward

A common mistake we all make on motivation is to assume that financial rewards are the most important and most motivating thing we can offer. The truth is—and this might be hard to accept because it is counterintuitive—that money has very little motivating effect beyond a certain point. So long as the wage is fair, anything over that such as special bonuses or massive cash competitions has very little additional impact on employee motivation. People love getting it, sure, but it can even be counterproductive because the payment of large bonuses tends to condition staff to only ever put in extra effort if they can see a wad of cash in it for themselves. Pay too little, however, and money becomes an astonishingly important demotivator.

Those retailers with the most motivated workforces have observed that offering significant cash rewards in exchange for performance improvements has three effects:

- ▶ It drives too much focus into short-term revenue generation at the cost of falls in customer service quality.

- ▶ It conditions employees to only go beyond the job description when they are offered a cash incentive to do so.

- ▶ Bonuses become absorbed quickly into the employee's general budgets and as such are not remembered over the longer term.

There is a whole filing cabinet full of research that suggests that cash triggers only very short-term satisfaction in the mind of the recipient. It boils down to cash being, by its nature, ephemeral—here today and gone tomorrow. I know you probably still don't believe me but this effect has been observed time and time again. Money is important but it doesn't create long-term motivation. You might need just to trust me on this one.

Money is important but it doesn't create long-term motivation.

Incidentally, you can measure employee motivation by looking at factors such as employee satisfaction, employee turnover rates, and customer service quality scores.

The stick to your carrot—implied sanction

Implied sanction is the stick to your reward carrot. It is the rulebook. It's "implied" because you may never have to use it but the team knows you would if pressed. It's "sanction" because it's what happens when the list of minimum standards is not met. Implied sanction is a strong motivating factor but one that requires significant skill to manage effectively. It takes a lot of common sense too, and certainly sympathy with the concept of "treat others how you would like them to treat you."

A sales assistant, for example, needs to know that a drop in customer satisfaction will lead to a serious chat. Furthermore, they must know that the serious chat will generate a set of actions that, if not carried out, will cast serious doubt over their future in the store. That's the sanction part.

The team needs to know that sanction is possible, but at the same time they must not be working in paralysed fear of that sanction. It's a tricky balancing act sometimes but much better than the alternative, which is to manage by fear. Management by fear generates lots of problems such as decreases in service quality. Frightened staff don't work well with customers. Fear can also lead to increased employee turnover and even industrial disputes.

In the 1980s, hard-bastard macho managers dominated retail management. Fear was a powerful motivator then because unemployment hung over pretty much everyone all of the time. Times have changed; there have been retail vacancies going unfilled for some years now. Management by fear is a poor technique, but we must recognize that we're all human. A lack of sanction for those times when we let standards slip lets us become lazy. To motivate, you must ensure that the team knows you have set standards for a good reason and that you will maintain those standards vigorously.

Successful one-to-ones

When you have to actually use sanction, be quick, be clear, and be fair. Here's the best format for a one-to-one in which you have to discipline a member of your team:

▶ 10 minutes to explain the general principles of the situation.

▶ 5 minutes to very specifically discuss the weakness or failure of the individual.

▶ 15 minutes to then explain why you have faith in that person's ability to turn around the situation. This is time to rebuild that person's belief in themselves and their abilities. Make sure you finish the meeting with the person feeling on a high.

You can probably see a lot of the 1-minute manager in that process, and that's fine. This is the practical way for retailers to do the same thing. Over the years, a number of store managers have recommended variations on this method to me, but I'd like to specifically credit Umesh Vadodaria for this version.

Treat me like a grown-up—self-respect

The default position for the majority of workers is to do the best job we can. If you create the right conditions, most people will work hard to deliver a good result. What stands behind that reality is self-respect. I've already talked about how the best teams are built on respect, and self-respect is a crucial component of that. It's what makes people feel like it's worth making the effort.

The opposite is also true: Put individuals into situations where they are robbed of their self-respect and they will react accordingly. People will steal and treat customers with contempt, and why not? If you take away somebody's self-respect, how can you ever expect that person to in turn respect your customers?

Without getting horribly political, I'd like to ask you to take a look at what poverty and unemployment do to communities. Take away jobs, put people in shoddy housing they don't own or ever could, then crime, drugs, and malcontent flourish. The truth is that if I don't respect myself, I'm not going to respect you. You can do such a lot as a store manager to encourage self-respect to grow among the members of your team.

Share information

Tell the team the confidential stuff: state of the cash flow, company health, costs, losses, and profits. Show that you trust them with such sensitive numbers. Yes, some of it will find its way to your competitors, but the losses will be vastly outweighed by the benefits.

Delegate power

Allow team members to make decisions for themselves, especially on discounts and customer service issues. Give people the confidence to make these decisions by ensuring that you have a good set of practical and sensible guidelines in place. Good procedures help people to make good decisions.

Delegate responsibility

Make members of the team responsible for the performance of specific departments. Responsibility is a powerful source of self-respect especially when combined with a variable such as profitability or sales revenue.

Encourage training

Make sure everyone who wants it has access to all of the training opportunities available. Make a habit of promoting manufacturer-sponsored training and seminars too. These are often of a high quality and they make a welcome break from the usual company formats. You are saying to the team members who go on these courses "I value you and I want to give you access to skills you'll find useful."

Share the good jobs

Make members of the team responsible for specific tasks, especially those "cushy" jobs managers sometimes keep for themselves.

Dive in

If you expect the team to polish and dust, do it yourself too; show that it is not a job that's "beneath you."

Listen to both sides

When a customer complains, listen to both sides of the issue. Don't blame the salesperson in front of the customer; you are responsible for service quality, so you make the apology. Then go talk with the salesperson and if there really is an issue, give them an opportunity to suggest ways in which to solve it.

Don't wash your dirty linen in public (even if you run a dry cleaner's)

Never embarrass or dress-down a colleague in public. I once observed a frustrated manager in Sainsbury's having a go at a cleaner in front of customers. This cleaner had been skipping work, but that didn't matter; the manager ended up looking like a bully. That reflected badly on the shop.

Consider the rulebook

Is there anything really daft in the rulebook that just forces people to do stupid things? If there is, then get rid of it.

Let others do the talking

Give everybody who wants to a chance to run team meetings. Encourage staff to present ideas at these meetings too. Go with the three-slide rule to prevent meetings becoming too competitive or boring: one to set-up the "what it is," one to explain the "how it is," and a final slide to summarize "why it is."

Listen

Shut up and listen to what people are telling you before you go making up your mind. Ask questions and allow people to give you the whole story. People respond better when they feel they are being listened to.

Encourage every opportunity for feedback

Get and give feedback on ideas, interviews, worries, suggestions, and concerns. Do this in an honest, active way. Take things on board. If the answer to an idea or issue is "yes," then get on and do it. If the answer is "don't know," go find out what you need to know. If the answer is "no," explain why. Offering a shrug and a "because it just is" is never acceptable. Always do these things within a short time frame.

Build people back up

If you have ever have to pull somebody up, discipline them, or criticize their performance, then always build that person back up again afterwards. Leave people on a high—if instead you send them back onto the shop floor feeling poorly about themselves, that will show.

Don't badmouth people

Every time you say "so and so is an idiot" in front of your team, you send a negative message about your attitude to colleagues. Negative talk infects your team—just don't do it!

Negative talk infects your team—just don't do it!

Recognize contribution

Learn to give specific praise as well as specific criticism. This is really very hard to do at first but is the most powerful motivating force of them all. Recognition is free and makes a real difference. By giving recognition, you are giving person X a reason to feel that "getting out of bed and coming to work today was worth it." The keys to recognition are to be specific, to do it as soon as you think about it, and to do it little and often.

Celebrate success

Absolutely essential to the strength of the team is making time, and plenty of it, to celebrate success. I don't mean the embarrassing forced stuff such as ringing a bell every time somebody makes a sale. Celebrating success means saying "well done" to people. It means making a small fuss of good things in the daily team meetings. It means going off for a pizza or a beer together. Toasting a hard-won target feels great. It feels even better if you've talked one of your suppliers into paying for the beer.

People need to know that the effort they've put into achieving something had a point to it. Celebrating success is one critical way in which you can do that. It says "I'm proud of us, we took on a challenge, and we beat it together." I cannot stress enough that you will gain many times more benefit from putting aside a proper budget for doing this.

Be ready to admit your own mistakes

If you get it wrong, be honest about it and move on: "Okay, I got this wrong, now how can you help me to do this right next time?"

Put the customer at the center

Show your people that you respect them by showing them that you're all working together for the same boss: the customer. It is the customer that we really work for. They are the ones who pay our wages. Teams need to have focus and in retail the customer is the best target for that focus. Everything you do must be built around the notion of helping customers to leave the store with a smile on their face.

Let's have a laugh now—using non-financial rewards

"Non-financial rewards" is just a name for the fun stuff. They can include all sorts of things such as extra days off, gift certificates, freebies, and holidays. Now there is a really, really, fine line here between exciting and tacky. It's so easy to make rewards embarrassing. Worse, lots of retailers go for the big dramatic holiday-type incentives where only one person can win anything significant. Maybe the best-performing store manager gets to go to Bermuda for a vacation. I've often worked with clients, employing thousands of people, who have insisted on running these demotivating incentive structures. They launch huge incentive programs worth big money but concentrated into maybe only five major prizes. Fantastic for the lucky five but really all this succeeds in doing is turning off the thousands who are pretty sure they won't win. Worse, out of the 200 who think they are in with a chance, 195 high-achievers are left feeling positively demotivated when they don't win that holiday.

When it comes to all motivating rewards, including cash bonuses, recognition, and non-cash bonuses, little and often is best. In this case, "little" because that means you can spread the budget much further and in doing so touch far more people. "Often" because it keeps things fresh and gives you lots of opportunities to boost performance without incentive programs going stale.

It's how you use the little non-financial rewards that's critical. As either an owner of an independent or as a chain-store manager, you have lots of freedom to do what you think will work best. Buddy-up with the manufacturer's reps. Let them do some training at your store one evening and suggest they give the expense account a workout by taking the team for a pizza afterwards. I'm always pleasantly pleased by how consistent manufacturer's reps are in this regard. They always say "yes" eventually.

As an owner of a store, you should be doing these things anyway, out of your own pocket. Incidentally, building in an ideas session before you eat is a good way of recouping the cost. I understand too that running a little meeting like this before eating has a positive effect on how you later have to account for the expense tax-wise, but check with your accountant in case I've got that wrong.

The wrong way to use non-cash rewards is to over-hype the reward or to use inappropriate rewards. So, for example, offering to give someone a CD for doing 200% of their target is an insult to you both. Wrong too would be to make a shy person stand on a chair to receive a commemorative "Top Guy" plaque. Use your best judgement and knowledge of the individual— what works for one might well turn off another.

Buy the team a gift each at Christmas but hand-write a thank-you note on each package. It reminds people that they are important to you. Always generously mark people's birthdays, weddings, and new babies. Preferably do so out of your own pocket rather than via a staff pitch-in.

Try to include your employee's partners on social invites. Partners have a massive influence on your people and on their view of you. A career in retail features strange and challenging hours that take people away from their families. Don't make that worse by extending this exclusion to the team's social occasions. Getting partners involved in idea generation can be very effective too.

Shopping is fun; we should all remember that.
Source: Koworld

Great non-cash incentives produced out of almost nothing

A good tip is to save any freebies you receive as a manager and pass them on to the team rather than keep them for yourself. Some managers save up these goodies to use in one go. Others dish them out right away. Either way, you must ensure that you don't fall into either of the following traps:

1   Only ever giving stuff to the loudest members of the team because they are the ones you notice.

2   Showing favoritism to a person who the team could, conceivably, suspect you of having more than a professional interest in.

Here are two ways of avoiding these freebie pitfalls and at the same time bringing some fun to the proceedings.

Team ballot

Say you've been lucky enough to find yourself with four bottles of champagne, two boxes of Belgian chocolates, and a stack of good promotional T-shirts. It happens! Over a week you have the team agree to nominate a colleague each for a thank you. All they have to do is write down the other person's name and a line on why they should be thanked. The key to participation is that anyone who doesn't make a nomination is disqualified from winning a prize themself.

Then you all pile down to the bar after close-of-business one evening. Get a round in, then read out the "thank-you" notes. Everyone who has been nominated gets to choose a random envelope. Try to make sure that everyone who should have been nominated *has* been nominated. Inside each envelope is a note telling them which of the freebies they've earned.

This is effective because the team sees that you could have held on to all the stuff yourself but preferred them to have it—people love that, they really do. Asking them to select worthy recipients gets people focused on their place in the team too. Team ballots are not heavy affairs but they really do work—aim to run one every six months or every quarter at a minimum.

Balloon day

This method of giving away all your freebies can be hilarious, great fun, nicely competitive, and very motivating. On one of your busiest days you fill your office with balloons. Each balloon contains confetti and a little envelope that has the name of a prize in it. To spice things up a little, I usually throw in some envelopes with fivers in them and some with a token for something silly like a coffee in them. Then you draw up a big chart with the names of all your team on it.

Now you need to set a challenge. Challenges can include such things as:

▶ To sell a specific item

▶ To gain an "excellent" score on a customer service questionnaire (do this as an exit survey, having someone stand at the door with a clipboard gathering answers)

▶ Selling add-ons, scoring a point for every transaction that includes a legitimate add-on ("legitimate" meaning the add-on was actually something that the customer will have been glad to have been sold)

Each time a person completes a unit of the challenge, they earn a "pop."

You can also award random "free pops" to members of the team, especially to anyone who isn't actively involved in selling. Do this whenever you observe a positive behavior. Those positive behaviors could include such things as solving a customer complaint or helping out a colleague. Each time a person earns a "pop," they get a token. These tokens are sticky and you can encourage people to stick them on the poster as the day goes on.

At the end of the day, after the punters have gone home, everyone gathers outside your office. Maybe you open some refreshments to help get the team revved up for the popping to commence. Starting with the person who has earned most "pops," you let each person into the room to pop the number of balloons they've earned during the day. Then they get to keep whatever falls out of the balloons.

I've run this one many times and it always gets everybody going. It's nice too if you can make the balloon day coincide with a team night out afterwards too. There are lots of variations on this theme such as having the prizes in lockers or in a sandbox and so on. I'm sure you can think up some yourselves too.

Recognition and motivation

Each of the motivating factors we've gone through here does in itself also have a recognition component. Giving out prizes is recognition, trusting somebody to make decisions is recognition, and bonuses are also a form of recognition.

Team meetings

In the previous pages, you'll have seen how important communication, team-building, recognition, respect, and trust are. One of the most useful opportunities to make things happen in these areas is your daily team meeting.

Yeah, I said "daily" team meeting.

I recommend you hold a 5- to 15-minute team meeting every single day. You don't have to do this but all the best retailers do. It's hard to build a team spirit if the team never gets to stop to spend a few minutes focusing together. Equally, what better way is there to swap ideas, to jump onto opportunities, and to share responsibilities?

Daily team meetings are the missing ingredient in many an otherwise great store manager's repertoire. Grab your store schedule now and write five headings into tomorrow's date and run a meeting around those five things. Some of the items worth covering in team meetings include:

Daily team meetings are the missing ingredient in many an otherwise great store manager's repertoire.

▶ Customer service issues and how these were solved

▶ Forthcoming events

▶ Promotions

▶ New products just in

▶ Bargains identified

▶ Review competitor activity

▶ Review new best-practice ideas identified

▶ Discuss incentive schemes

▶ Review any challenges

▶ Introduce new employees

▶ Review targets and performance

▶ Celebrate success

▶ Recognition

▶ Consider improvement ideas—even if you can only do this one, it will have been worth having the meeting—the next section talks you through how to find loads of these ...

Please do this daily—I don't mean to nag, and I know shifts and part-timers and such mean you'll need to juggle a bit, but the effect is hugely positive. You're a leader, yeah? You can only be that if you set down plans, review those plans, and keep everyone up to date with what's going on and what's expected of them.

8

CHAPTER EIGHT

All we need is a little better every time

Ideas are the fuel for organizations. What you do with those ideas, how you convert them into action and improvements, is what then makes the organization grow and prosper. Space for improvement can be readily found in all areas, especially in technique, systems, presentation, recruitment, and performance. All retailers can benefit from a culture of everyday performance improvement but few try to. Don Taylor and Jeanne Smalling Archer, authors of the very helpful *Up against the Wal-Marts*, call this "kaizen," as does Julian Richer in his awesome book *The Richer Way*. Others use different names for the same thing. Kaizen is Japanese for "continuous improvement involving everyone."

I don't think we need to slap a Japanese jargon word onto the making of improvements. For me the task is as simple, and as vital, as "let's do it a little better every time." That sets up a very simple question for your team members: "How could I do this again but even better?" Your mission statement comes in here because it helps define what "better" means for your organization.

Improvement in this sense isn't necessarily about massive earth-shattering changes. What we are looking for are those everyday improvements: improvements in the ways in which we look after each other, our relationships with customers, and the quality and relevance of our processes. A typical example might be the discovery that one piece of paperwork can be integrated with some other process rather than be dealt with separately. Combining the two will save money and time—so that's an improvement.

It could be the realization that the rules of a promotion we've created can be simplified to the benefit of the customer, and that is an improvement too.

Gathering improvement ideas

You will need to have two things in place:

1   A way to gather ideas.
2   An improvements slot on the agenda for discussion at team meetings.

If you were to look at just one task or process in each daily team meeting you will have 7 improvements each week, 30 for the month, and 365 over a year. That's awesome. Okay, so maybe you won't get into this every day but you will still generate a significant store of improvement ideas every month. Working in this way is easy. You are not attempting to change the world in a day, you are just looking to change one little thing at a time. Every journey starts with just a single step—remember that.

Every journey starts with just a single step—remember that.

Do you currently change anything each month? Does change only ever happen dramatically once a year? "Let's do it a little better every time" puts you in the driving seat of change. Your team becomes a valuable engine of change.

Statistics can make you go blind—the measurement trap

Plenty of otherwise sensible people believe that you cannot improve that which you cannot measure. That's dangerous, wrong even, and here's why: Some of the most effective customer satisfaction-improving tools are un-measurable in a conventional sense. Smiling at a customer turns out to be one of the most effective ways to make them feel better about you and your company—how do you measure the number of smiles your team gives out?

Here's something to think about: a number of aspects of sexual perform-ance can be measured. Factors such as duration, the dimensions of various body parts, room temperature, heartbeats per minute, can all be easily recorded and measured (you might need somebody with a clipboard to come in and write this stuff down for you though). But do any of these factors automatically add up to guaranteed great sex? Of course not.

Measuring the wrong things is a real trap. This is a grim example but its worth telling; a U.S. Army general noticed that the daily success of the Vietnam War was being measured by relative casualty rates. A measure as crude and unpleasant as "if we kill more of them than they do of us then we must be winning." Convinced this measure did not convey a useful picture, this general instead created a set of metrics that also took into account territory, specific objectives, and economic cost.

It is what the general said about his reasons for doing this that is absolutely relevant to retailing. He said, "We are only making important that which we can easily measure when instead we should be measuring only that which is important." Just because you can measure unit sales easily, for example, does not make that the most important part of your business to concentrate your improvement efforts in. Customer satisfaction is harder to measure but far more important because it relates to unit sales made today, tomorrow, and next year.

Case study 8.1 Not Smart Retail: The classic measurement mistake

In the early 1980s, the Coca-Cola Company had become incredibly twitchy about the strengthening performance of Pepsi, their nearest rival. Pepsi had made big strides into Coke's market and one stat, in particular, had the execs at Coke sweating: in 1972, 18% of drinkers said they drank Coke exclusively against just 4% choosing Pepsi. By the start of the 80s, this ratio had moved to 12% favoring Coke exclusively and 11% Pepsi.

And that's when Pepsi pulled its genius move and unleashed "The Pepsi Challenge." Pepsi targeted committed Coke drinkers and presented them with two small cups of cola, one marked "Q" and one marked "M." Almost without fail, drinkers would take a sip and choose "M"—which would of course then be revealed as Pepsi.

Initially the team at Coke attempted to claim that Pepsi's campaign was fixed. But when they then ran similar experiments themselves, they ▶

discovered a 53% to 47% split in favor of Pepsi. For the market-leader, this was a bombshell—the impact of a six percentage point spread could be measured in millions of dollars in potential lost revenue.

The team were horrified and commissioned a slew of additional market research projects. Each came back with similar results and attempts to qualify the choice for Pepsi began to suggest that Americans had fallen out of love with Coke's distinct "bite." What was once described as "refreshing" became "harsh"; the same tasters began to associate words like "smooth" and "rounded" with Pepsi and went on to suggest they preferred these attributes.

Roy Stout was the head of Coke's consumer marketing research team and is the man who made the connection between losing market share and product taste. He reasoned, "If we have twice as many vending machines, have more shelf space, spend more on advertising, and are competitively priced, why are we losing [market share]? You look at the Pepsi Challenge and you have to begin asking about taste."[1]

This bombshell drove the board at Coke to make an extraordinary decision—they would change the hitherto sacred and world-famous secret Coke recipe to take account of the perceived change in America's cola preferences. And thus was born "New Coke," which had a lighter and sweeter taste, a taste more like Pepsi in fact.

Early test results were good—New Coke pulled level with Pepsi on blind tasting preferences. A little more tinkering followed and New Coke began to pull out a persistent 6–8% lead. The board then took the decision to take it to market and launched a massive campaign behind the new formula.

All the research said New Coke would be a winner.

It failed and failed dramatically. Tens of thousands of Coke drinkers rose up in protest, sales of the new drink faltered, and, cutting a long story short, the company were forced into a humiliating climbdown and reintroduced the original formula as Classic Coke. Very shortly afterwards, sales of New Coke all but evaporated.

Why?

The flaw was, in hindsight, a very simple one. Coke has a predominantly citrusy-burst flavor, whereas Pepsi has a more raisiny-vanilla taste.[1] Take one or two sips of Coke and the experience is quite sharp, the bite is very strong; do the same with a can of Pepsi and the first gulps are much smoother, sweeter, and gentler on the palate.

But! Drink a whole can of either cola and the experience changes completely. And this is the flaw—Coke drinkers like the way a can of coke tastes, but they don't entirely like the first few sips. Coke drinkers who prefer the first sips of Pepsi when tested blind, often complain of a cloying sweetness when they then go on to drink the whole can.

New Coke is a fantastic example of an entire company both putting too much emphasis on the research and ignoring instinct and emotion. So what were the real reasons for Coke's slipping market share?

Consensus of opinion is that Coke had allowed their marketing spend to mature along with their product. They had failed to sell to the younger, hipper, cola drinkers Pepsi had become so adept at communicating with. Coke's customers were leaching away to a preference for coffee and later bottled waters whereas Pepsi's were still enjoying rotting their teeth on "The Choice of a New Generation."

I'm not entirely discrediting management by numbers, but stories like this one go a long way to proving that without the emotional context, you don't have the full story.

---

[1] Stats and background information taken from *Blink* by Malcolm Gladwell (Penguin, 2006).

Go with your gut feel

Use your gut feel and allow yourself to apply improvements even to those processes, tasks, and interactions to which you are unable to attach numbers. I'd like to ask you to consider valuing the power of your gut feel more highly. Gut feel isn't random. It's a guide, an instinct that tells you a certain path may be the right one to take. It is also that good sense which tells you not to do something. But it needs tuning: Books like this one exist to help you separate out correct gut feel judgements from other emotional factors such as fear or laziness.

Even science is now beginning to come round to seeing gut feel as something real and valuable. There is a credible theory that suggests decisions made on gut feel are more often than not the carefully calculated result of our experience and knowledge and that instinctive gut feel decisions get better as we add new experiences and knowledge to our memories. Think of your gut feel as a potent business weapon, a weapon that is unique to you.

Think of your gut feel as a potent business weapon, a weapon that is unique to you.

I wish I had more space here to go into instinct and gut feel in more detail but you want to read more about shops and that. Luckily there are already two brilliant books out there you can read instead: *Blink* by Malcolm Gladwell (Penguin, 2006) is really good at explaining the process at work in instinct-led decision-making and *See, Feel, Think, Do* by Andy Milligan and Shaun Smith (Marshall Cavendish, 2008) is even better at helping you to build your confidence in using gut instinct to make decisions. If you only fancy reading one, get Andy and Shaun's—it's really very, very good and you'll get a lot from it.

Making improvement work for you

Let's do it a little better every time. As well as running through ways to apply this idea at team meetings, you will need to create an environment in which the team feels comfortable to try things, and to suggest things. If you are the kind of person who greets every new idea with "I'd love to change that but …" or "I can't see that working" then soon people will stop trying and suggesting. Equally, if members of the team feel that you are likely to discipline them for making mistakes then no one is going to want to try anything new for fear of punishment.

Get the culture of improvement established. Allow your people to question how they do things and you will benefit enormously. Make that an everyday occurrence: little steps but lots of them, and you and your customers will feel those improvements take hold.

Room for improvement

The best retailers do not stand still when successful. They strive to keep the momentum, to keep growing and to keep moving forward. That growth and movement is inspired by tiny little everyday improvements just as much as it is by sweeping change.

Here are some of the categories in which you will always be able to find lots of opportunities to improve things. The thoughts listed here are a deliberate mix of actual ideas and of pointers to get you looking in the right places for ideas of your own.

You might like to pick out a single line during daily team meetings and have the team come up with some thoughts and ideas on that theme.

Improvement and customers

▶ Consider everything from the customer's perspective.

▶ Encourage customers to tell you their complaints (the most cost-effective research you'll ever do).

▶ And listen to them sincerely when they do.

▶ Think about the type of people who come into your shop—who are you missing?

▶ What do customers prefer about your competitors (ask them)?

▶ Talk to customers all the time (ask staff to tell you one thing at each meeting that they've heard from a customer).

▶ Aim to improve average transaction values.

▶ Use eye contact more.

▶ Walk your store like a customer would.

▶ If you can, get hold of former customers and ask them why they don't love you any more.

▶ Use email, Twitter, Facebook, YouTube, and similar to communicate with customers; it's cheap, powerful, and very direct.

▶ Whenever you are resolving a customer complaint, ask customers how they would improve your service.

▶ Remember names.

▶ Think carefully about the integrity of your pricing.

▶ Send them stuff they might actually like to see.

▶ Where can you add value to the customer experience?

▶ What can you promise today that is better than yesterday?

▶ Run surveys.

▶ List the benefits of doing business with you and then tell customers about these benefits.

▶ What do other people do well that you really ought to be ripping off for yourselves?

▶ List all the things in your store that regularly delight customers—then think about how to double the list.

▶ Are you leading by example?

▶ Write down a list of all the processes that touch customers directly—all of them.

▶ Then do a list of all those that don't—can you strip any of these out?

▶ Make it easy for customers to give you feedback—use the internet, suggestion boxes, receipt surveys, telephone aftercare calls, open evenings, and everything else you can think of.

▶ Get customer opinion on new products before you put those products into your range.

▶ Ask customers to tell you "what's missing."

▶ Ask customers to tell you what they like about your store.

Improvement and you

▶ Read stuff.

▶ Get involved in the business community—join your street or shopping centre advisory committee or the chamber of commerce.

▶ Talk to your business neighbors.

▶ Ask people about your management style (and listen openly when they tell you).

▶ Learn from those below you as well as above you.

▶ Seek out examples of great retailers and learn from them.

▶ Sign up to every Internet resource you can find—here are three useful sites to start: www.theretailbulletin.com, www.nrf.com, and the fashion-biased but still very useful www.Racked.com. Equally, there are loads of great retail Twitter feeds—mine is called TheseRetailDays, if you would like to hear more from me.

▶ Get a subscription to *Retail Week* and learn to read between the lines. (Why did so and so make that choice? Why is X thriving? Why is Y on its uppers?)

▶ What things do you do outside of work that might be useful inside?

▶ Make an honest list of your strengths.

▶ Then one of your weaknesses.

▶ Go on courses.

▶ Sign up to every training and seminar resource you can initially—the more you go on the better you will become at recognizing which ones are going to be truly useful in future.

▶ Naff as it might seem, set life goals and then yearly goals for yourself—what do these goals tell you about the areas in which you will need to concentrate personal improvements?

▶ Listen to people more than talk to people.

▶ Open your eyes!

▶ Go shopping more often—do things your customers do.

▶ Read the trade press.

▶ Learn from competitors.

▶ Learn from people outside your sector.

▶ Maintain your standards.

▶ Get rid of the "yes" men and surround yourself with people who challenge and inspire you.

▶ Appoint an honest and strong assistant manager—they will soon let you know where you have room for improvement.

▶ Improve the balance of your life: You look after shops—shopping is fun, try to see it more that way.

Improvement and colleagues

▶ Reward people for improving things.

▶ Consider issues from your team's perspective.

▶ Don't get mad with people for trying.

▶ Let grown-ups think for themselves—empower people to make their own improvements.

▶ Encourage talk, talk, and more talk—leave every feedback channel open all the time.

▶ Give people a look at these lists.

▶ Buy employees a copy of *Smart Retail* for Christmas—remember to wrap it up nice; in fact, get your Dad a copy too, and all your friends.

▶ Recognize people's contributions.

▶ Don't rip off your staff.

▶ Never criticize employees in front of anyone else.

▶ Build a great culture founded on trust and respect.

▶ Tell people you are upset with them whenever they make you feel that way.

▶ Are your job descriptions a jargon-filled sack of nonsense?

▶ Feel free to build friendships but never forget that you are the boss—keep a perspective.

▶ Encourage the team to be open with mistakes.

▶ Have a laugh together.

▶ Always, always celebrate success.

▶ Be human in your relationships—if someone is going through a life crisis help them cope with it.

▶ Share the numbers—let the team own them as much as you do.

- Pay a profit-related bonus.

- Pay a customer service-related bonus.

- Smile when you walk through the door every morning even if you don't feel like it.

- Make sure everyone knows about all available courses and seminars.

- Put aside cash for training.

- Let good people go on courses you've been on—use training as a reward.

- Be specific with instructions.

- Sales assistants get closest to your customers—listen to what they tell you about those customers.

- Challenge people and encourage them to challenge themselves.

- Teach by example.

- Show people that the best way to do things is to consider solutions rather than dwell on problems.

- Get the team involved in all the big decisions.

- Help employees to see that it is customers, not you, who pay their wages.

- Hold regular one-to-one appraisals but be prepared to allow employees to tell you what they think of you, of your business, and of the team too.

- Have a team meeting every single day—just 15 minutes' worth but make those minutes count.

Improvement and costs

- Take a firm and consistent line on employee theft—always fire proven thieves and prosecute wherever possible.

- Walk the fine line between minimizing customer theft and creating an unappealing high-security atmosphere.

- Prosecute shoplifters.

- Anything the customer doesn't see only ever needs to be functional and cost-effective—but don't short-change staff on a place to eat their lunch or get five minutes to sit down and catch up.

▶ Try to get stuff done right first time—especially the solving of customer complaints.

▶ Negotiate everything.

▶ Pool resources with your neighbors.

▶ Swap cost-saving ideas with them.

▶ Keep track of all supplier rebates and discounts.

▶ Tell the team when you're close to earning a rebate and explain what needs to be done to get there.

▶ Get more than one quote!

▶ Find the special group rates negotiated by your trade association.

▶ Listen to what customers tell you they think is important—anything they don't rate highly is probably not worth spending so much cash on.

▶ Cut out the middleman wherever you can.

▶ Recent design graduates are a much better and more cost-effective option for your advertising and direct marketing than an ad agency is.

▶ When placing print orders, or booking a TV or radio ad, always demand the agency discount—this is a 10–20% discount that printers, radio stations, and TV channels give to agencies; just because you book direct doesn't mean you shouldn't get the discount too.

▶ Make good use of government employment programs but listen to your conscience—if it looks like slave labor, it probably is slave labor.

▶ If an employee isn't pulling their weight and you have tried hard to help them, you have to let that person go.

▶ Do any members of the team have any skills that might mean you can avoid hiring in a tradesman? Pay the employee a proper bonus for any above-and-beyond jobs that they do though.

▶ Be sure that you understand how your customers have found out about you—improve or cut any activity that is not driving traffic.

▶ If you pay employees a profit-related bonus then that will in itself help limit some of the unnecessary expenditure—so long as you are also sharing the store profit-and-loss information.

▶ Use your ideas program to harvest all the cost-saving ideas the team can come up with.

▶ Consider sharing savings with the employee who identified them.

▶ Be nice to suppliers and let them pay for stuff if they want to.

▶ Get rid of the waste—any process that does nothing for customers, or for you, just has to go.

▶ Look at these processes all the time.

▶ Reuse things whenever you can.

▶ Teach employees how to promote the business when they are outside of work.

▶ Ask the team if they know a way to get hold of something cheaper— years ago when we bought a horribly expensive color photocopier, it wasn't until the behemoth was delivered that one of the warehouse workers said "New copier? I could have got you a discount, my Dad's regional director for Canon."

▶ Talk to your landlord as much as you can, get a relationship going, and negotiate support when you need it.

PART THREE—**CUSTOMER**

Make me happy and I will give you my money.

Source: Steve Bowbrick

CHAPTER NINE

We love shopping here!

Give customers the best possible experience when they visit your store—that's how you'll make more money. There—the most blindingly obvious sentence in the whole book! Yeah, of course such things as cost control, the basics of margin, and pricing have to be right too, but the starting point for everything we do in retail is the customer. How they feel about us, what they want from our stores, and how we meet those needs. Sending customers out of your stores with a big smile on their faces, a smile that lasts through getting their new stuff home and using it, is your absolute priority. So, how do we paste that smile on their happy chops? Read on, my friends, read on!

Great customer service

I often talk about how customer service isn't an add-on activity—that great service quality comes from everything you do as a retailer. Some clients, understandably, feel that I'm hiding the secret to great service quality … well, thing is, there isn't one. What I can do here though is to point out more of the places in which you can work to create overall improvements in the customer experience.

That word "experience" is important: Great customer service is made up of lots of individual customer experiences and I much prefer using the word "experience" rather than "service." It's not a nod toward consultant blather—I reckon it's easier to understand how to improve things if you think at the individual level: "What can I do for each individual customer? How can I make their specific experience of my store a great one?" But when you talk about service, it feels like a nebulous thing—it's general and non-specific.

First and foremost, it's worth talking about why most initiatives focused on service quality fail. Sometimes a marketing team will take a look at their list of "things to do" and one of the bullet points will read "make customers love us again" and they'll commission an agency, or two, to come over and create some sort of "service event." They'll then have good fun taking this event around the store estate and they'll say to people "we order you, albeit in a nice way, to smile at customers and be their friends and love them so they will love us."

And these one-off initiatives often deliver big early uplifts in customer satisfaction—then those gains die off, usually quickly, and before long everything returns to normal. That's because the focus always moves on—no matter how committed a retailer is to raising customer service quality, there is always another issue waiting in the wings to occupy the minds of management and teams.

Permanent improvements in standards of customer care have to be earned from the ground up—you can't change things by layering initiatives onto unstable foundations. Building from the ground up is harder work but ultimately more satisfying because gains become self-sustaining and permanent. Dieting is a good analogy—crash dieting creates instant weight loss but almost always results in a net weight gain once the focus slips. Changing eating behaviors, seeking support, changing attitudes to food, and learning about nutrition means slower weight loss but, for the vast majority, permanent and self-sustaining success.

"Self-sustaining" is the key phrase—a successful assault on changing the behaviors and relationships that lead employees to *want* to deliver great customer care becomes a positive viral thing: Changes feel good, staff get more from their employment experience, and customers get more from shopping the store. Even better—these changes reinforce each other in a virtious circle:

Happier staff → better customer experience → happier customers → better interaction with staff → happier staff … and round and round.

Better still, that loop delivers gains in revenue and profit and draws in improvements in employee retention and reductions in employment costs. It is an absolute win-win.

One team at a time

As a store manager, you might now be thinking that there's nothing you can do to influence levels of service quality in your store, that it's all down to centrally dictated policies. Well, you can influence service standards—your leadership is absolutely vital in creating a good place to work and in filling it with a motivated team. Doing that, following the advice in the "Team" section of the book will make a massive impact on how it feels to come and shop your store—with all the benefits that generates. You might have some weird service rules in the business, but you as a leader are making customer experiences into great ones.

Where things get tricky is in navigating your way through the negative stuff that sometimes you're asked to implement. A great example of this was seen at electrical retailer Powerhouse before that business, funnily enough, got into serious financial trouble and went bust: at one point staff were forced to ask every customer if Powerhouse could please sell them their gas and electric. It was really pushy—staff felt uncomfortable and customers absolutely loathed being asked.

And then they went to Comet or Currys instead.

Faced with something like that, as a manager, what do you do? To be honest, the right thing when it gets that extreme is to read the writing on the wall and jump ship. For most of you though, any negatives impacting on the employment experience, and therefore the customer experience, will stem from good old-fashioned well-meaning but poorly informed policies—unforeseen results of otherwise sensible decisions. Your role as a manager is to try to make these work, at the same time as feeding back your experiences and explaining why such-and-such isn't perhaps the world's greatest idea. Get customer and team comments, show you have tried to make a policy work, and create a compelling case, with alternative solutions in it. Then talk to your bosses.

We need answers on this customer service thing

I know, I know, you're still thinking I'm on a cop-out here. Right, here's a bunch of stuff you can do to make sure that you and your team are delivering great customer experiences and that you send your customers away delighted.

Employee satisfaction

I've probably gone on a bit about this but it's worth saying again: Put into practice the stuff in the "Team" section of this book—the most effective way to ensure your team is delivering more great experiences is to improve the satisfaction of your staff. Having a reward and bonus program based around customer satisfaction scores can be really effective too. It helps your team to make a direct link between how they look after customers and what goes into their own pockets.

Simplify

Be simple and straightforward for customers—make promotions easy to understand and simple to redeem. Use plain language in your advertising and communications: Be clear about what you can and can't do.

Deliver on the promise of your Big Idea

Whatever that Big Idea is, it is also a promise to your customers that you will be what you say you are! If a customer is coming to your store expecting you to be this Big Idea, then make sure that you really are and keep looking out for all those things you could be doing that serve to support and emphasise that.

Meet the fundamental discovery need

All shopping is about discovery (see "Store" section): Help your customers to make those great discoveries. Surprise, delight, inspire, and wow them. Be proud of your stock, make heroes out of the amazing and brilliant, and, above all, make sure your people are knowledgable, that they have access themselves to your product and that they are open-minded enough to listen to customers" real needs and then to find great ways to meet those.

Be consistent

Make sure your team are on top every day—make sure you exceed company standards, stay on top of your game. And across the company ensure that the experience is great, in every store, every time.

Fix problems directly

See, the thing is—any one of us could end up on *Watchdog* one day with Anne Robinson's curiously wonky face looming as she tells us that we are the devil incarnate. That's just the way the world is, but we can reduce our chances of this happening by accepting that we will make mistakes sometimes and then by getting on and fixing those problems quickly, fairly, and with a smile.

Feedback

Making it easy for customers to give feedback to you is critical in improving service quality. If you haven't got a customer complaint process, one that's easy for customers to use, create one. Give customers quality surveys that they can fill in and send back to you. Give them prepaid envelopes to make it even easier for them to do that. Give out your email address and watch for Twitter mentions. Encourage complaints and think of them as free market research. Some customers will rant and rage but at the heart of almost every complaint is a truth that, once learned, will help you to make your business better. Oh, and it's far better that customers complain to you, and that you resolve their complaints, than it is for them to complain about you to their friends instead.

> **Encourage complaints and think of them as free market research.**

Be honest and open

If you don't know the answer to something—say so and then find out. Be ready to admit your mistakes and involve your team and your customers in fixing things and in improving the store. Have an open mind in all situations.

Don't pay sales commission

Put your people on individual sales commissions and some of them will shark your customers. That's simple, straightforward human nature. The best service organizations pay people bonuses based on customer satisfaction combined with something reflecting overall store-profit performance. Or just be a great employer and give your front-line people salaries. Some of the happiest, most satisfied customers in the U.S. are customers of The Container Store: "Our salespeople do not work on commission; instead, they're either salaried or paid by the hour with wages far above the retail industry norm. Therefore, they often work together in teams to find that complete solution for the customer, which allows them to spend as much time as necessary to help customers find what they need." That's simple retail right there.

Smile and be nice, dammit!

Okay, I'm not talking the pained smile of the retail damned—but do try to put your troubles to one side when dealing with your team and your customers. Use the great opportunity you have as a retailer to talk to people, to enjoy their company, and appreciate the fact that you're not stuck in an office staring at the same ten faces all day every day and fearing your turn on the coffee run. Retail is ace like that—for every mean-spirited or rude customer, you'll work with a hundred who are good fun, who are loving being out and spending money. Shopping is fun—have fun yourself, you old misery.

Respect your people and they'll respect your customers

Treat people how you yourself would like to be treated. Be nice, be respectful, give the benefit of the doubt, and remember that your people are grown-ups. Treat your team that way and they'll do the same with your customers.

Living and breathing it

Every decision you make must be in the context of "will this be good for our customers?." Every person you hire must be someone you think customers will enjoy being served by and every process, promotion, and event you choose must be for the benefit and delight of customers. Delivering great customer experiences is not a bolt-on activity—it is the only activity. Every word in this book is written in the context of great customer service.

If experiences are poor, business will suffer. Customers have less patience for poor service than ever before and have even learned how to complain. If there *is* one secret to delivering great customer experiences, it is the knowledge that great customer service begins with your people.

If experiences are poor, business will suffer.

Great moments

What are those great customer experiences? What do they look like? I tend to feel that it's mostly about empathy, common sense, turning on and off the cheek and the banter at the right time, delivering on your Big Idea, and making sure people leave your store with smiles on their faces. Here's a bunch of examples of great customer experiences culled from our customer panel. Almost all of them are pretty ordinary but in each case the effect on the customer is huge: big enough for them to (a) remember it and (b) to bother to write about it on a forum. In each case, these are customers who will favor the stores involved again.

Lush—Sheffield (UK)

Nathan Ditum's experience

> I went in to buy a birthday present for my sister-in-law, loaded down with a stroller (Maddy) and a hyperactive four-year-old (Jay). One girl in there was really friendly and polite—it didn't feel like she was being pushy, just helpful. She helped me choose a gift pack for the gift (as a regular customer, I know Lush's stock, but she knew all about which was best for sensitive skin, hairtype, etc.) and to choose a bath bomb as an extra for Sarah. Jay's been in before and he loves taking the bath bomb samples and watching them fizz up—this ace girl not only got some water out to occupy him so he wasn't buzzing around the shop while I was looking around, but added a sample of his favorite one into the bag for free, and then even dug out a baby one for Maddy.
>
> Jay and I were chatting about how nice she was all the way home. It's the sort of customer service encounter that—small though it is in the big scheme of things—puts a big smile on your face and can make your day.

Myer—Adelaide (Australia)

Pete Muller's experience

I got a tip-off from my brother that Myer had 20% off TVs. Seeing as the retail price for the Sony I had my eye on was $5k, I was pretty keen on saving substantial coin. Unfortunately, I couldn't make it in on that Saturday, and wandered in on Sunday instead.

Oh, said the sales guy, it's only 15% off today, not the 20% we were running yesterday ... but since you knew the deal was yesterday, I'll give you the 20% off anyway. Unnecessary, I thought—after all, it's my fault I didn't get in yesterday—but nice, and definitely appreciated. I take the sales guy's card, and arrange delivery—unfortunately, 5 weeks away.

A couple of weeks later, Sony announce a deal where a purchase of one of their TVs garnered you a free PlayStation 3 if you sent the receipt off. Damn, I thought, bad timing on my part ... but I thought I'd chance my arm and see if I could get a receipt re-issued with the appropriate date on it. Went back into the store, saw the same salesperson; he remembered me. I asked whether he could re-issue the receipt: "No problem," he said, "we'll just refund and re-purchase your TV, you won't even lose your place in the line." (There was a massive backlog of this model, hence the 5-week wait.)

Refund, then. "We'll issue a refund onto your credit card, but that'll take a couple of days to go through; if you can deal with double-dipping on the credit card for a couple of days, that'll be great." Unfortunately, my card was damn near maxed, and couldn't accommodate another $4k hit. "That's okay," he said, "we'll issue the refund in gift cards, then scan those cards back in for the purchase."

That's when I discovered that Myer only issued a maximum of $500 on one of their gift cards, meaning he had to initialize and re-scan 9 cards. The whole process took nearly 45 minutes (due to the laborious nature of the gift certificates), but he remained cheery throughout—which I thought was fantastic, especially since he'd already got his money off of me.

Specsavers—Cheltenham (UK)

Melanie Taylor's experience

… sat on my metal-framed glasses a while ago. Annoyed that I'd have to wear my spare pair for a few days, I went with the broken ones in hand to Specsavers in Cheltenham, from where they were purchased. It was a Sunday morning and the store was pretty busy.

"I've sat on my glasses," I said. "Do you think they look fixable?"

The lady at the front desk examines the severely bent glasses. I fully expect her to say, "They might be too bent to straighten out again," but instead she says, "Yes, no problem at all."

"How long will it take?" I ask, thinking I'll have to come back after work the next day, or even later in the week.

"Oh, we're a bit busy—could you come back in 20 minutes or so?"

"Oh! Sure!"

When I return to pick them up, the store is still very busy. The same lady immediately turns to pick up my glasses as I approach the counter. "Here you are!" she says brightly, passing my glasses back. They have been so well repaired they look like a brand-new pair. I am amazed. "How much will that be?" I ask, digging in my pocket for a tenner. "No charge!" she says. "We don't charge for minor repairs if you bought your glasses from us. Would you like a slip case for your spare pair?" and she hands me a soft case so that I can take my crappy old pair home without scratching them.

Now THAT'S what I call good service! And that's why I have gone back to them to try contact lenses.

The Warehouse—Christchurch (NZ)

Sty Smith's experience

A few weeks ago, I was trawling through the CDs and DVDs on special offer at this no-frills giant store. I came across a *Riverdance* DVD—knowing that my wife likes *Riverdance*, I decided to buy it for her, especially as it was on at a bargain NZ$15. The DVD wasn't the original one released when *Riverdance* was first launched but was a more recent show filmed in Geneva with different dancers.

While I was paying I mentioned to the girl at the counter that I had really been looking for the original version but this was a good deal anyway. She then said that she was sure they had the original in somewhere for the same price. She checked the computer and confirmed that it was indeed in stock and then spent ten minutes with me searching through all the places it could have been out on the shelves and in the bargain displays, all to no avail.

She then very kindly offered to keep an eye open for it and give me a call if she came across it: She wrote down my phone number and that was that for a couple of weeks. I then, one day, got a very clear message with her name, the store, the fact that she had located the DVD and had put it aside for me for a week, and I could come in and collect the film when it suited me.

That felt like proper service and I've felt good vibes about that store ever since.

Center Parcs—Longleat Forest (UK)

Nick Taylor and family's experience

It's a very big operation so I was very much expecting it to be rather impersonal, or the staff to have the noticeably false "smile and say nice things to the customer" manner that had been drummed in at training sessions. But from the very first person we met on arrival the feeling I got from the staff was genuinely warm, helpful, and enthusiastic.

Then through the stay, it was obvious that really careful planning had gone into making things run smoothly and hassle-free; for example, I was expecting to have to stand in line on the day we had to return hired bikes, but there was extra staff on hand to speed things along at the time when there would be highest demand. All of whom seemed to be enjoying what they were doing and were very helpful and friendly. We might have just been lucky, but to me it felt like it was the culture of the place, and we're going back this Christmas.

Anthropologie—New York (U.S.)

Chris Ahchay and Sarah Treacy's experience

We'd bought some jeans and that from Gap, wandered out of the shop and off on our merry little way without really thinking anything more about it. As you do. Unfortunately Gap had forgotten to take the security tags out of our clothes so in the next shop we went into we set off their alarms.

Now, maybe it's just indicative of what I've come to expect in a big town (a shrug of the shoulders and a cursory bag-search if you're lucky) but the security guy in the shop took one look at the Gap bag, said "Oh, that'll be the security tags then, they're always doing that." He then sent one of the shop girls to find a pair of scissors and then spent five minutes carefully unfolding our Gap stuff, finding the tags, and cutting them out, before folding them all up again and sending us off on our way. All while having a perfectly pleasant conversation with us about our stay in New York and what not.

We bought some candles.

Ship & Pilot—Ilfracombe (UK)

Neil Meddick's experience

Wandering around trying to find a pub with proper ales, I was glad to see six options available and the pleasant man behind the bar offered tasters of the two I had my eye on. Went for a splendid pint of Exmoor Beast, in a handled glass to boot. On returning my glass to the bar and thanking him, I continued on my way.

I didn't then go back for nearly two weeks, but on entering I was greeted with a knowing "hello" and asked if I would like to try the new barrel which was similar to the one I had tried on my previous visit. He then told me what ales he was having on in the next three months and the exact dates they would be available. He then continued, explaining how he kept his ales exactly as per CAMRA. It's one of those places that makes you want to go back because its obvious they care about what they sell and they create a friendly atmosphere. Brilliant, really brilliant.

Two local banks—Pennsylvania (U.S.)

Steve Trimble's experience

I spun a yarn some years ago about Mellon Bank not wanting to give me a plush lion stuffed animal, because I was an "existing" customer and that the plush toys were for "new" customers—it was a nice stuffed animal that I thought my then young kids would enjoy. I closed my account and took all my money out, then opened up a new account with a dollar, got the stuffed animal, and then closed this account. I then walked over to Wells Fargo and opened up an account there out of spite.

Well, yesterday I found myself in Wells Fargo standing in line waiting to do some banking, when I noticed they were giving out ceramic piggy banks. I thought my youngest boy would just love to have one. Not only do I have a personal account, but we have four business accounts with this branch. After my banking needs had been dealt with, I inquired about the gift and was told it was for new customers opening up new accounts. I then asked what about their old customers—and then it happened! She smiled, asked if I wanted one and actually gave me one! Then a wink and a whisper, "just don't tell my boss" ... completely excellent! I'll bank there forever ...

Elliott loved it and spent a good part of last night racing around the house gathering spare change for his bank ... good customer service rocks!

The Natural Grocery Company—El Cerrito (U.S.)

Thomas Moyles's experience

Was picking up some ingredients for sweet potato casserole and wasn't having any luck finding chives. One of the ladies working there smiled and said something nice about my baby son and made it obvious that she was available to help without pressing it on me. When after a few more minutes of poking around I did ask her, she showed me where the packaged chives were as well as the fresh green onions if I preferred to go in that direction.

At the check-out line, both the lady working the register and the bagger fawned over my son and were very friendly and when I was about to put the cart back while carrying my son, an employee jumped in and said "Let me get that for you, sir." Nothing big, just a pleasant experience to go in to a store and have lots of friendly people creating a comfortable feeling—I really did just have a bit of a happy glow going out to the car.

People make the difference to great customer experiences

Of course, what rapidly becomes apparent in a service business like ours is that you can only look after the customer by looking after your staff. So, the route to creating value for the customers is through management of your people. Good retailers always understand this instinctively and we, at Tesco, regard it as a major priority.

Sir Terry Leahy—CEO, Tesco.

Quote taken from the fantastic *Uncommon Practice* by Andy Milligan and Shaun Smith (Financial Times Prentice Hall, 2002).

This year, I pledge my loyalty

Customer loyalty is a myth, a consultant's pipe dream. A nonsense. Trying to gain it, trying to buy it, trying to bribe customers is ridiculous, costly, and pointless. A customer is no more loyal to Top Shop than she is to New Look. She'll happily shop both of a Saturday afternoon. Incidentally, Tesco Clubcard and Sainsbury's Nectar are called "loyalty schemes" but they aren't really, they're customer data v. rewards programs. You let us understand how you shop and we'll give you a few tokens as a thank you. Tesco, in particular, have been able to do great things with that data. It's a worthwhile exchange.

So, some of us might be loyal to our brand of breakfast cereal or toothpaste but we are not loyal to the names above the door of the various places we can buy them from. But even that brand loyalty is moot in an age when choice is ubiquitous and consumption predicated on disposable living. Sure, personally, I've never forgiven Colgate for discontinuing my favorite sub-brand of toothpaste and actively seek out remainder stock of the green nectar from discount stores (I have 20 packs in reserve right now— thank you, Home Bargains in Liverpool) but if Macleans come up with a toothpaste that tastes and performs as well as the green one—it's so long, Colgate, and not a second's pang of regret will be felt.

This is the reality, my friends. Time to find a new reality—and here it is.

First-visit advantage

First-visit advantage is a move on from the blunt definition of customer loyalty. Traditional customer loyalty holds that customers will always come to you to satisfy their needs in your product areas. To the exclusion of all other stores. Nonsense. The world doesn't spin like that.

But what if we can build formats so great and customer experiences so compelling that people are prepared to give us the first opportunity to sell to them on any given shopping trip? So compelling that they will come to you first before moving on to your competitor's stores. There is loads of evidence, including really strong stuff from Paco Underhill's Envirosell team that shows a massive percentage of customers will buy, or return to buy, the first item they really like on a shopping trip. And common sense says getting the first crack at satisfying customers" needs is a good thing.

The idea of first-visit advantage is that customers enjoy the experience in your store so much that whenever they plan a DIY project, or want to buy some clothes, or want to make something nice for lunch, that yours is the store they visit first. They may park their car nearest to your store rather than a rival's, or visit your retail park before moving on. Being given first crack of the whip leads to a much greater probability that the customer will buy from you in preference to a competitor.

It is a very powerful concept.

First-visit advantage can be won in three ways: through promotion, through preference for your format, and through the human experience in your store. Remember especially that the human parts of that equation are always the most powerful.

Human interaction is bricks-and-mortar retail's secret weapon.

As retail trainer Kate Phillips pointed out (I promised I'd credit Kate with this bit, so I have), there is one area of loyalty that does still mean something to customers: loyalty to people. And she is of course right—wherever you have the opportunity to build something personal, there's a chance that people will respond very positively to that. It's not about forced smiles and pretending—it's about developing a store culture in which staff feel comfortable to chat with customers, to share honest opinions on product, and to banter and be themselves. Much of what the "Team" part of this book tries to do is to support exactly that type of culture—it's very valuable if you can do it. It's also one thing a traditional bricks-and-mortar store can do better than one online—never underestimate the power of eye contact and a genuine smile.

Case study 9.1 Smart Retail: Becoming first

One of Europe's leading DIY businesses discovered in 2006 that customers were only putting 20% of their total project spend with that retailer. Customers were actively driving to these stores, parking the car, walking down the aisles, and still only actually spending a fifth of their cash for that project at that store.

Big chunks of their project budget was found to be going to specialists in tiles, flooring, kitchens, bathrooms and gardens. Customers only came to these huge DIY sheds for the extras, cheap offers on base materials, and for tools.

A legitimate interpretation of that situation would be that customers were almost begrudging having to give this retailer even that share of the project spend.

The response has been to make big investments in improving the in-store format of those specialist areas, bathrooms, flooring, etc., and in significantly raising standards of customer service. To an extent these changes are now paying off; however, I believe this particular retailer needs to do much, much more on service standards before it can undo its losses to the specialists (and that's why I've not named the retailer in this case study).

The four rules of performance improvement

There is no secret to performance improvement. The techniques can all be learned. But just as some racing drivers can make an identical piece of metal move consistently faster than that of a teammate, so it is that some retailers are able to improve performance better than anyone else. I've known a few racing drivers over the years and the best of them have one thing in common: consistency of line. They take the right line through more corners more times than anyone else. That's it—nothing magic or secret or unknowable. The same thing holds true when it comes to performance improvement. There is no secret; it's about getting the details right and paying attention to the fundamentals—checking you're consistently hitting the right line.

The rules of performance improvement are so beautifully simple and there are only four of them.

To improve performance you can:

1   Sell to new customers.

2   Sell more in each transaction.

3   Persuade existing customers to return to your store more often.

4   Improve margin by cutting overheads and improving sales quality.

This is another of those "it's not rocket science" moments. The challenge is of course in understanding how best to apply each rule. The chapters in this section of *Smart Retail* deal with those things you can do to produce direct results from applying these rules to your customers. People and store issues also have a part to play in the successful application of these rules, of course, but it is what you can do directly for the customer that has the most significant impact.

Priorities

If I was forced to choose just one of the four rules of performance improvement over all others, the one I would pick is number two, "Sell more in each transaction." Driving up average transaction values is all about maximizing every opportunity. That in itself is a powerful business improvement philosophy. "Make the very best of every customer who walks in" is your first consideration.

Driving up average transaction values is all about maximizing every opportunity.

Added value

Everyone wants a bit of something extra, something free, or on top—a bit of added value. Where we retailers sometimes misunderstand that is to think that added value needs to be made out of actual "stuff." Customers place value on the less obviously, umm, valuable too—the convenience of a local corner shop is added value, for example, and in certain circumstances a customer will happily pay a little extra for that added-value convenience.

In black and white here the list below feels very ordinary—it *is* pretty ordinary as it goes. Where the magic happens is in the way in which you and

Where the magic happens is in the way in which you and your teams put this stuff into practice.

your teams put this stuff into practice. A "tip sheet" sounds a bit dull—but written with passion, fun, energy, and a bit of wit, it can be a really welcome part of the customer experience. Do these things consistently and have them support your Big Idea and they carry significant power.

Here's that list:

- ▶ Recommendations
- ▶ Product demonstrations
- ▶ Masterclass technique demonstrations
- ▶ Product training for customers
- ▶ Tip sheets
- ▶ After-sales service
- ▶ Trade-in
- ▶ Expert staff
- ▶ Credit facilities
- ▶ Loan product availability
- ▶ Pre-order facilities
- ▶ Services such as tailoring
- ▶ Specialist product ordering
- ▶ Delivery services
- ▶ Free samples
- ▶ Try-before-you-buy
- ▶ Convenience
- ▶ Design services

Case study 9.2 Smart Retail: Value equations

Staff cost money and sometimes it's easy for retailers to see the wages line on a profit and loss account only in terms of the hard figures. At a store committed to everyday low prices at all costs, the percentage of revenue budgeted to cover staff costs might be as low as 4 or 5%. One such retailer is The Home Depot, whose big idea is so entrenched in the idea of everyday low prices that it might not be able to afford to trade at all if it had a wage percentage much beyond that. Now that's fine when you're incredibly far ahead in an exponentially growing market (as Home Depot were in the 90s U.S. DIY sector)—frankly you could force customers to wear T-shirts printed with "I Smell" and they would still come to you for low prices and wide ranges. What Home Depot has been experiencing for some while now is the effect of a flattening market—all of a sudden, customers start to subconsciously add things like service, advice, inspiration, and shopping environment to their personal value equations and that's why Lowe's, who appears to invest more in training and service, picked up customers so rapidly.

What I need—what I want

We've talked a lot about understanding customers and that's because it's fundamentally important—they have needs and we have to understand those needs and steer our businesses and the customer experiences within them toward those needs. So here's a neat thought exercise that will help you to get a clearer picture of what those needs are.

It's a tough exercise, this one—I always ask my clients to brainstorm those needs and to write down as many of the possible needs they believe their customers might possibly have. Instinctively most retailers kind of know what these are—but articulating them is a struggle.

So why bother? At its most basic, understanding the most likely of your customers' needs makes it easier for you to sell stuff to those people through the addressing of those needs.

The first bit of this exercise seems a bit silly at first but try it before reading the "answers." Try to do this in a group if possible—better ideas tend to emerge that way.

Needs Exercise Part 1 | Glass

Fetch a drinking glass and put it on the table in front of you. Set a timer for five minutes and then write down all the things you think that glass could possibly be used for. Pick it up, handle it, think about what you could do if you broke it.

Done live, and in groups, the longest list of different uses I've had is 54.

Reveal:

Okay, time's up: Take a look at your list, look at the progression of uses on it—you'll have uses like "drink out of it" and "pen holder" up near the top and then, closer to the bottom, the mad stuff will appear, such as "anti-burglar device (smashed in a doorway)" and "wasp prison."

Okay, more analysis on that in a moment, but first you need to do part two.

Needs Exercise Part 2 | Shirt

Do the same thing as with the glass but this time use a shirt instead.

Reveal:

Again you'll have a nice mixture of obvious "wear it" and lateral "to create an instant disguise." Now, what I'd like you to do is to look at both lists and next to each use write down a need that use could satisfy. So with the glass and "drink out of it," the need might be "to quench a thirst." Then do the same again but this time add a second "need" to each line. So you might then have "drink out of it"—"quench a thirst" plus "to wash down some aspirin."

Those second ones are much harder to do but still represent a legitimate need. Take a look at the lists—the "uses" there can be thought of as your customers" actions "Bought a TV" or "Inquired about contact lenses," and the needs are, well, needs. So you might have "Bought a TV"—"Because I was impressed by 3D" plus "I'd like to watch football in 3D."

These first two are all about getting your brain unlocked, so now move quickly on to the really important stuff . . .

Needs Exercise Part 3 | My Store

Now, with unlimited time, write down all the possible things customers could use your store for, including listing all the different broad categories of products you sell and services you provide.

Then take five of those "uses" and for each of them list at least ten "needs" that your customers could possibly be satisfying by using your store for.

Needs Exercise Final Part | Action

By now you should be buzzing with real customer needs—let's have a crack at using that to learn something useful about our store.

Choose a section of your store or a particular range of items.

Consider:

▶ What are the needs of customers shopping this section?

▶ How are we satisfying those needs?

▶ How does this fit with the Big Idea?

▶ What needs are going unsatisfied?

▶ How clear is our added value in this area (if this applies)?

▶ What can we change to meet a wider range of needs, to better meet existing needs, and to improve the performance of that part of the store?

CHAPTER TEN

Price and value

I've not gone into theoretical strategy much in this edition; I have in the past but I reckon now that it's not useful to generalize. There is one area of strategy that *is* worth talking about though and it's pricing. It's worth talking about for a handful of reasons—one primary one is the value of bargains. Bargains are brilliant in almost every store—upmarket boutique or down-and-dirty pound store (I love pound stores, incidentally—Poundland, especially, is a fantastic example of focused and thoughtful retailing).

Everyday low prices (ELP)

Everyday low pricing is an interesting modern pricing technique. It's also the best example of the failure of slavish dedication to a rigid price proposition. The theory of ELP is that every price in store is as low as possible every day. Furthermore prices will not be slashed during sale periods—indeed there will be no more sales at all, just the lowest prices every day.

U.S.-based Wal-Mart is often credited as the pioneer of ELP. Founder Sam Walton would almost certainly have suggested that all Wal-Mart did was to take discounting and direct-from-manufacturer purchasing further than his competitors.

I worked for Comet when the company first introduced ELP in the late 1980s. A Kingfisher finance team attempted to codify ELP into a philosophy and then to interpret it as a mission applicable to the whole business. Pricing became the absolute focus of what we, as a retailer, did. To make pricing the absolute mission was wrong, and I'll explain why as we go on.

I am always mistrustful of attempts to shoehorn simple common sense into complex strategy. At Comet we interpreted ELP as meaning all prices would be monitored against those of major competitors, then adjusted to match or beat these price points. In addition, each key product category would feature at least one product priced lower than any entry price-point offered by our competitors. The product would then remain at that category-killing low price everyday. So, for example, we offered a 14" portable color TV (remember those!) at $99 when the previous entry price-point for this product was $109. All our competitors were at the $109 price, so we were a good chunk cheaper. For how long do you suppose that competitive advantage lasted? A year? A season? Well, Dixons, Currys, and Argos cut their price point to match ours within days. All that happened was the whole sector now made $10 less profit for every one of those 14" televisions sold. That's $10 lost out of gross margin, don't forget.

Because we at Comet were committed to our misinterpretation of ELP it made it very hard to respond in-turn to our competitors" actions. If we dropped our own price further, it would have damaged the credibility of our ELP proposition, suggesting that our previous price was not the lowest everyday price after all. If we remained at $99, just like everyone else, we had no competitive advantage since pricing had become our only competitive lever. Building the mission around ELP provided no competitive advantage at all. Comet's current CEO, Hugh Harvey, has spent the last handful of years trying to move Comet off price-focus and on to a proposition based around service—I hope he manages it but with Best Buy breathing down Comet's neck in the UK ...

When rivals" store environments, prices and product ranges are so similar there is a terrible fear that a customer will simply walk from store to store and buy on price alone. Comet, as do many others, believe that convincing the customer that their prices are always reliably low will ensure the customer only comes to them. I'm not sure that's very realistic given the amounts being spent on a single electrical product. Would you only check one store when spending $800 on a TV? No, nor would I. ELP, as practiced by many, is fatally flawed.

Would you only check one store when spending $800 on a TV?

Merchant dealing

I put the challenge of the $99/$109 14" TV to a number of Britain's best retailers. They decided quickly that it would have been much more effective to have taken that TV and to have slashed a genuine deep cut off the price, say to $89, and then to have run that as a limited stock promotion. We would have negotiated a larger order with our original equipment manufacturer (OEM) and taken a bigger discount. That stock would make up the limited promotion. The promotion would then have been presented honestly to customers: "Here's a fantastic deal we've negotiated specially for you—once it's gone, it's gone." Indeed, in the second half of the last decade, this is exactly how Asda and Tesco have been beating the electrical retailers at their own game.

Yes, the competition would still match our price but by then we would have enjoyed at least two weekends of price leadership in this category. Also, competitors would be forced to cut their margins from existing stock bought at their usual cost price, so their profit per unit would actually be less than ours.

This bargain $89 TV would feature heavily in local press and radio adising. Customers flicking through the local paper would see a bold, bright, honest ad. Many customers would bring forward an intended purchase as a result: "Let's get one now and put it away for Tommy's Christmas gift" and "You've been on about a TV for the kitchen, shall we get one while this cheap deal is on?" And a significant number of customers would switch to Comet for this purchase because:

1   We made it easy for them.
2   We gave them a good reason to act now instead of tomorrow.

I strongly believe that real competitive advantage comes from maintaining honest everyday prices mixed with bargains. Quite simply: not ripping off the customer, and retaining the ability to offer great, customer-delighting, promotions. It is this approach, call it a philosophy if you want, that will enable your store to convince customers that you are honest people to do business with and that you are capable of exceeding their expectations on price.

Making bargains the star

Back in 2007, I got this nice note from Irish book retailer Lyn Denny: "I'm the owner of a small independent bookshop in Ireland. We've been open a year and things are going great. I bought your book in September and haven't looked back. We immediately introduced a bargains table and it has been the fastest-selling area of my store ever since. We are delighted with it and so are our customers." Apart from me showing off a bit, why this is worth talking about is that Lyn's store isn't some downmarket discount shop: Bookstór (www.bookstor.ie) is a quality independent in a country that values literature highly. People love bargains and they work in almost any store. Oh, and Lyn's store is still with us—look at their website and you'll get clues why: The store is buzzing with energy, it's not just books on shelves. There are story events, loads of communication with customers, passionate and inspirational recommendation, and loads of character on show.

Even in a chain-store branch where you don't get to dictate prices you can still make bargains the star. There are always awesome offers in the price lists—these might be end-of-line items or even regular stock. Try pulling lots of the end-of-line product into your store from other stores around the company and then putting them out there in front of customers. Don't forget clearance and manager's specials too as bargains.

Make up some simple flyers featuring these star bargains. Hand these out on the car park and around town. If you have budget, get them delivered with the local free papers too. Have your team point out the specials to every customer who comes through the door: "Just in case you're in the market for X later, I wanted to tell you we have got them priced at Y for a week or until the stock runs out." That's not pushy; it is friendly no-pressure selling.

Enthuse the whole team at your daily team meetings. Tell them about the day's top three bargains. Consider running a little incentive on those lines: A bottle of champagne goes to the person who sells the most over the weekend. A bottle of bubbly is just enough to help the team to take notice; it's a welcome treat for most, but it's not so much that salespeople will mis-sell just to get it. Put flyers on doors and on the counter top. Set up an A-frame outside if you can. Sometimes the council take offense at the presence of these A-frames, but you won't know until they send you a nice letter and ask you to take it down, so go ahead and see what happens!

Pulling together the bargains is hard work. You must be inventive, on top of your inventory, and ready to act fast. The work is worth it: You will drive customers into your store and the combination of honest pricing and real bargains will boost your reputation and your sales. Bargains give you competitive advantage.

Bargains give you competitive advantage.

Case study 10.1 Smart Retail: The democracy of bargains

In 2007, Primark, a proper no-nonsense bargain high-street fashion retailer, opened a 70,000 sq ft flagship store on London's Oxford Street. Hilary Alexander, writing in the *Telegraph*, described the scenes on its first day: "I have never seen anything like it. Even the first day of Harrods" sale is a vicarage tea party compared to the Primark pandemonium. By 11:15 a.m., there were still crowds three and four deep winding around the block on both sides and spilling onto the roadway as a mounted policewoman appealed for people to 'please stay on the pavement.' Security guards estimated tens of thousands had arrived by midday."

That mention of high-class department store Harrods is interesting— I've visited the Primark store a number of times since it opened and the customers in there are broadly the same people also shopping Selfridges, Debenhams, John Lewis, Next, and Gap on the same street. The only customer group missing in Primark from those stores are the wealthy over-50s. Thing is, a Harrods customer is as keen on a bargain as anyone else. The millionaire enjoys being able to boast that he got an extra diamond set into the face of his new Rolex Oyster for free, just as much as we do when we manage to snag a second bag of mini-peanuts on a flight. That's what Wal-Mart, Primark, and even Bookstór are tapping into: the buzz customers get from beating the system, from getting a real bargain. All customers love bargains—we are living in a bargain-driven culture.

Cost and value aren't the same thing

Lots of retailers are able to create a premium positioning and charge a bit more for the things they sell. That's obvious, but I wanted to take a closer look at some specific examples and get to grips with how those retailers are able to make customers feel comfortable paying a premium.

Selfridges (London), Bloomingdale's (New York), Galeries Lafayette (Paris, Berlin)

Every last thing in the beauty departments in these four stores can be had for less by searching for thirty seconds on the Internet. Yet those departments, even in trying economic times, generate huge sales and profit. Why do customers spend in this way? For the theatre, the fun, the demonstrations, the quality of the advice, the convenience of being able to try things and ask for samples. Oh, and if you stand in these four (and I'm sure other department stores too) you see that the vast majority of shoppers are not super-rich posers, they are the ordinary boys and girls working in the offices locally and enjoying their bit of retail therapy.

The Container Store (U.S.)

Sell shelves to put things on and stuff to put things into, and other storage-related paraphernalia. Similar, cheaper products can be found easily—often right next door from Wal-Mart, Target etc.—yet this runaway success story was part-sold in 2007 for what was rumored to be near a billion dollars. This is an exceptionally successful store and that's because customers prefer to buy these products from the Container Store because they value the expert advice and the specialist nature of the store.

Lush (UK)

They sell soap. Soap is soap is soap—but Lush sells relatively expensive soap to people who will happily walk past the cheap soap in Tesco just so they get to make a second trip to a store that makes them feel good about themselves. We will look at Lush a couple of times in this edition to understand why that is—see the case studies under Big Idea and Format-led discovery.

Diesel Store (Global)

Again, Diesel jeans can be had from the Internet cheaply but the Diesel Store is not about price: Customers flock to these stores for the experience, for the feel of the store, to be able to touch and feel real product, and for the interaction with people excited by the product. Staff are passionate and knowledgeable: They will tell you about the denim and will chat enthusiastically about cut and fit and colors. Customers value that kind of experience in-store and are willing to pay the proper price for it.

Oi! That's my planet too—the costs of consumption

While we're on the subject of pricing, this is a good place to talk about the flip-side of the price-driven consumption frenzy. I'm one of those people who grew up in the 1970s and 80s in a world that believed consumption at any rate could be sustained forever—too young to be bothered by the early 70s oil shocks and too old to really "get it" when, late in the 90s, environmental concerns began to break mainstream ground. Ten years later and even people like me have been forced to confront the reality that the blue and green ball upon which we stand isn't going to last if we keep kicking the crap out of it. Parallel to that we've begun to better understand the long-life health benefits of eating better and walking about a bit more.

As retailers we are in the vanguard of consumption and we have some serious thinking to do. Here and now I need to say that I am an unashamed liberal-capitalist and I believe strongly that the creation of wealth is a force for common good in the world. I'm also very supportive of the idea of globalization: one planet, one nation—and why not.

So how does that square with the need for sustainability? Being one of the world's biggest sources of employment is a pretty good start—everyone is entitled to opportunity, dignity, and the chance to earn a decent wage. Retail provides that, and here's where we start to get to important stuff— time and time again it is proved that those retailers who treat their staff with respect and who provide support and opportunities for self-fulfilment are the ones that customers prefer to shop with. On the customer side, growing awareness of the need for sustainable living is leading a quiet revolution, with our customers taking more and more of their money to those retailers whose practices have the least negative impact on the planet.

We're really good, as an industry, at moving minds and influencing consumer behavior—I believe the most forward-thinking retailers have an opportunity here to move customers even faster toward truly sustainable consumption. Why wait for consumer trends and government regulation to push us? Let's drive that change ourselves—not just because doing so, on a human level, is a feelgood thing, but also because we can drive our business's success by doing so.

Broadly, there are two routes open to retailers driving toward a sustainable position:

1   Commit the entire format to a sustainable position (Whole Foods Market, Lush, Abel & Cole).

2   Operate a traditional business but introduce a significant commitment to sustainable practices (Marks & Spencer, Waitrose, American Apparel).

Making these moves is a good community choice and a great human one too. Of course, the usual caveats apply: Choose your position carefully, communicate it well, and above all be authentic—if you say you have a commitment to X then you must genuinely believe that commitment to be right or you run the risk of being "found out."

Case study 10.2 Smart Retail: Live it, breathe it, sell it

A key event in the early days of Whole Foods Market set the tone for the way in which this innovative food retailer sees itself as an integral part of the communities it serves. In 1981, a flood devastated Austin, Texas; among the businesses ruined was the company's then one and only store. The damage ran to $400,000 and without insurance they looked doomed. Incredibly, customers and neighbors volunteered to join staff in clearing up the mess and in repairing the store—creditors and suppliers too provided breathing space for the business to get back on its feet and, less than a month after the disaster, the store was up and trading again. Many people not employed by the company or financially dependent on it nevertheless felt they had a stake in the success of the business. If your local Tesco, ASDA, or Sainsbury's suffered a flood, would you be there bailing out and mopping up?

Right from the start, Whole Foods Market has had a clear vision that the food they sell should be grown responsibly, that local supply and the variety that produces, was preferable to the established mass-production model, and that employees and the community should be closely involved in the decision-making driving the business. They have a snappy line to sum up the way the business feels about its offer: Whole Foods—Whole People—Whole Planet.

What makes Whole Foods Market special is that they have made direct positive connections between "doing the right thing" and making money. Just one small example of that: They offer financial support to employees who choose to do voluntary community service—and they know that doing so makes both the employee and the community feel good. They also know that a happy, motivated employee helps the business to make more money and that an involvement with the community increases customer awareness. There is no cynicism in this: The top team wants to be proud of the way in which they do business; they want to go to bed at night knowing that their working day has resulted in gain for everyone and in the right way.

I'm sure too that Whole Foods Market would be happy to carry on at their own rate, expanding when sensible to do so, and to a large extent minding their own business—the world though has come into line with the principles driving Whole Foods Market and that should spark an interesting period for the business.

CHAPTER ELEVEN

Promote or die

Carefully considered promotions are important because they create interest and surprise, and in conjunction with honest pricing and added value, are essential performance improvement tools. There are of course those other factors we've talked about to consider—promotions in isolation from great customer experiences or attention to employee needs are near worthless. Poor, aggressive, or sneaky promotions may bolster sales short-term but unhappy customers will rarely come back (breaking Rule 3 of the four rules of performance improvement in Chapter 9—Persuade existing customers to return to your store more often) and will tell friends how awful you are (breaks Rule 1—Sell to new customers). Unhappy employees will leave (that has a cost to you, so breaks Rule 4—Improve margin by cutting overheads and improving sales quality) or will not make any active selling efforts (breaking Rule 2—Sell more in each transaction).

28 promotions

Here I have listed most of the popular promotion options. I've included a table that makes it easy to see which promotions are good for achieving better performance under each of the four improvement rules. Finally, the promotions planner that follows after will help you to see what promotions are right for you and when to run them.

1—Joint activity

Look for promotions you can share with either manufacturers or other retailers in your street. The obvious benefit is that you can pool costs and then afford to promote the activity more aggressively. An example of retailers engaging in joint activity might be a "fun day" held within your

So long as they walk out with a bag!
Source: Koworld

shopping center. A manufacturer and retailer joint activity could include manufacturer-supplied demonstrators, linked to a customer promotion and a manufacturer-funded staff incentive.

2—Displays in empty stores

I need to credit brilliant retail speaker Rick Segel with this great idea: Find the landlords of an empty local retail unit and offer to put a display in the window. It makes the unit look more appealing for the landlord to rent and provides you with an excellent adising space. I first mentioned this in 2003 when it was super-rare—you see it a lot now and it seems to work well for everyone involved.

3—Sponsorship and community events

Don't dismiss requests for sponsorship right out of hand. Sometimes a sensible sponsorship can do more for you than, say, your Yellow Pages ad. Businesses located at the center of smaller communities gain most benefit from this form of promotion. Sponsoring events such as the town fun run or village fete makes a very strong statement about your commitment to the community. Many retailers have reported that the goodwill this creates does translate into sales.

4—Ads in changing rooms

Cheap, easy, and brilliant: put ads in your changing rooms. Your customer is absolutely captive when they are in there and they have plenty of time to read. Think about featuring deals on accessories especially—customers who bite will be helping to push up your average transaction values.

5—Children's competitions

Maybe we are just a nation of soppy souls but children's competitions always work well. These can be very simple coloring competitions or letter writing. Perhaps themed "draw or write a letter about your Mom for Mother's Day." Local papers love this sort of thing. You have a good chance of getting a photo printed in the paper of the winner in your store.

6—Tip sheets

No matter what your product you can easily produce useful tip sheets. A sheet of tips might seem a little uninspiring perhaps, but time and again retailers tell me that customers go nuts for these, often citing the tip sheets as the reason why customers come back. You can write tip sheets yourself or have a well-known expert do them for you at a cost. Formats can be anything from a full-color booklet to a small card fixed to a shelf edge. My favorite format is loose A5 so that customers can take the tip sheets away with them. Here are some forms of tip sheets:

▶ Recipes in a grocery store

▶ Recommendations and explanations in a wine merchant's

▶ Hi-fi reviews in an electrical retailer

▶ Home projects in a DIY store

▶ Album reviews in a music shop

7—Loyalty programs

I don't believe that customers are ever loyal to the over-hyped special offers, magazines, or bits of tinsel that most loyalty programs consist of. In my wallet is a Nectar Card, a Tesco Club Card, and an HMV Card.

However, I'll happily spend money in Asda, buy songs from iTunes, or get a quart of milk from Mehmet's round the corner. I'm not loyal even though I am in the loyalty program. Neither am I alone in that response, but then, I think most of us understand that those schemes are really about data for benefits and we use them accordingly.

The kind of loyalty programs that work in more immediate ways are usually much simpler. Maybe a coffee shop gives you a little card that they stamp each time you visit, and that entitles you to your sixth coffee free. Or a pizza company offers a loyalty bonus that allows you to get any pizza you want for free if you have saved up four receipts from previous orders. Those kind of loyalty programs are unobtrusive and relatively low-cost and customers really like them.

8—Customer-get-customer

You could offer existing customers a gift, store coupons perhaps, if they recommend your store to a friend who then makes a purchase. All you need is a printed coupon, which you give to every customer with their receipt. The customer can fill in this coupon and give it to their friend. The friend brings in the coupon and it has the original customer's details still written on it so you can send them their reward.

If you are confident that people like you enough to recommend your store to friends, this is an effective way in which to make it easy for them to do exactly that.

9—Buy one, get one free (or two-for-one, three-for-two, etc.)

In the early 2000s, this was the UK's most popular promotional mechanic. If you can afford to run them, run them. Promote such offers heavily. Talk to your suppliers about funding either the offer, the advertising or both! If you can run a steady stream of good offers over a long period then this becomes even more effective because customers begin to pop in just to see what you've got on "special."

10—Sampler clubs

In some ways, this is an extension of the tip sheet idea but with a chance for customers to actually try the product out. You take a group of your customers and sign them up to a hands-on sampling club. In that hi-fi store example, you could hold regular demonstration evenings just for members, hold set-up lessons with an expert, make pre-ordering on limited edition products available to the members first, and run exclusive offers.

11—Percentage off

Exactly what it says: You run either a day where everything is, say 10% off, or you reduce a selection of lines for a limited period of time. It has become very hard to make such events really work though. The DIY stores especially have trained customers to think that anything less than a 25% discount isn't worth their while. Percentage-off promotions also make a negative statement about your usual prices.

12—Special nights

Inviting selected customers to join you in the store for an exclusive evening of demonstrations and offers can be very effective. Provide refreshments and snacks and if appropriate bring in a relevant speaker, and entertainment too. Try to pick a theme or a special reason for doing it because that can help you to more effectively promote the night. A sports shop, for example, could invite customers in to celebrate the England Football Manager's birthday. It's frivolous, sure, but gives you a hook too. This is another one that can get you coverage in the local paper.

13—Surveys

You should be asking customers for their views anyway but surveys can also be used as promotional tools. Create a survey and then mail it to members of your database. Include a "thank you" voucher for a discount in store. It reminds customers you are there, it tells them customer satisfaction is important to you, and it gives them a reason to come and shop with you.

14—Celebrity visit

Getting a celebrity into your store for a PA (public appearance) can be fantastic for generating traffic. They are not always as expensive as you might think either; TV actors, especially if they live locally, can be a bargain! You can find the contact details of almost all British-based actors in a book called *Spotlight*. Your town library will have a copy. Make sure you tell customers and the local paper that this is happening.

15 Book signings

You don't have to be a bookshop to hold book signings. A fishing tackle shop can get just as much benefit from having the captain of the British Course Fishing Team in to sign his new book. In fact, it's sometimes a good way for a non-bookseller to get a celebrity in without having to pay them. Heavily promoting the event is key to making a book signing really work for you.

16—Lunch at the store

People are so busy today that lunchtime often becomes a trade-off between eating and shopping. One idea is to help your customers to do both. Think about putting on a simple open-packaged lunch for every customer who visits you on one day or one week of lunchtimes. Obviously it's worth avoiding greasy or staining food. Leafleting local offices is the best way to promote these events. Word is that they are really very effective at getting new people into your store.

17—Seminars, "how-tos," and in-store events

Absolutely essential, whatever your business. Get local traders, designers and even manufacturers" reps in to show off your products and show what to do with them. Construct a series of seminars, "how-tos," and in-store events and then give every customer a calendar with these marked on it. Seminars attract customers and they help customers to decide to spend more money. "How-to" demonstrations and events such as fashion shows bring theater and drama into your store. That excites customers and helps to make their experience of your store a much more enjoyable and interesting one.

Seminars attract customers and they help customers to decide to spend more money.

18—Meeting place

If you have a training room or large office that is not fully utilized consider offering it to local businesses as an outside meeting space. This creates massive goodwill and hardly anyone currently does it, which will mean you will stand out. Maybe invest in a coffee maker and a lick of paint to make the place attractive. Check your insurance terms just in case.

19—Charity giving

An honest charity promotion is a winner in many sectors. Usual format would be to partner with a particular charity and then agree to donate a stated percentage of profits earned during a specific special charity day.

20—Local radio outside broadcasts

If you have got the space offer to let the local radio station come and do an OB (outside broadcast) from your parking lot or store. Make it coincide with a strong event and you'll find the stations quite interested in becoming involved.

21—Banded product

This is a cousin of the buy-one-get-one-free offers. Banding is usually applied to fast-moving lines and means either attaching a different product to another for free, or putting two products together as a package deal. It's a good way to move a slower line out with a more popular one and to please the customer at the same time.

22—Discount off future purchase

I am a big fan of this technique, also sometimes called "delayed discount." Every customer buying on the promotional day gets a money-off voucher that they can use in the store on another day. Usually the value of the voucher depends on the value of the original cost, so a typical offer might look like this:

▶ Spend $20, get a $5 voucher off next purchase.

▶ Spend $50, get a $12 voucher.

▶ Spend $100, get a $30 voucher.

You can afford to be quite generous because a high proportion of the vouchers you give out will never be redeemed. Incidentally make sure that whatever you use is secure and that it has an expiration date and a thousandth of one cent cash equivalent mark on it.

Promote it on the day with lots of bold signs and make sure you have told all your database contacts to come visit. This promotion type makes a great story for adising too.

23—Gift certificate promotions

Very similar to the discount-off-future-purchase offer except redeemed using normal store gift certificates, which can be used at any time. Customers treat gift certificates more like money, so redemption rates, and cost, will be much higher.

24—Buy now, pay later

A credit-based promotion. Very popular among big-ticket retailers because it enables customers to fulfill tomorrow's desires today! Actually they are a good deal for both shopper and retailer. These promotions don't carry perhaps the same excitement and call to action that they once did, though. Customers are used to seeing them now. Like the store card I'll mention in a bit, be careful to make this a good, honest offer rather than something that ties people in debt they can't cope with.

25—Interest-free credit

A very powerful promotion that enables customers to buy your product and pay for it in installments without them incurring any credit interest. Various deals are available to suit independent retailers and are worth serious consideration if you are aiming to move big-ticket items. Same considerations as in number 24 apply.

26—Store card

Store cards earn us retailers a lot of money, and they can be very convenient for some customers. I struggle with store cards though from an ethical standpoint. This is a very expensive form of credit with interest rates that are way above those for ordinary credit cards or for personal loans. Lots of good ordinary people, our customers, get caught up with by store cards and they run up huge debts with awful consequences. Retail is a people business—I don't believe we should be responsible for making anyone's life more difficult. So for that reason I cannot recommend running a store card.

27—Time-limited

At 4:00 p.m. all bread rolls free with soup for half an hour. Every Monday shoes are 20% off. On the hour, every hour, this Saturday we will offer a different item in limited stock at a crazy price. Great for creating instant interest and PR. In the last example, if the stock is too limited then you do risk annoying customers. Amazon.co.uk's 2010 "Black Friday" promotion of this type generated masses of bad press as offers sold out fast, often in under a second.

28—Bargains (price promotions)

And finally, the most powerful promotion of all: the humble bargain. Customers love bargains—so much so that I have filled this book with thoughts on how to get hold of, promote, and sell bargains in your store. Scour your price lists, badger your suppliers, pester the marketing team, gather up end of lines or last season's stock, and go mental for your customers. Bargains bring people in: They make them spend more and they bring them back again.

> **Bargains bring people in: They make them spend more and they bring them back again.**

Table 11.1 Promotions and the rules of performance improvement at a glance

The scale runs 0 to 10 0 = No effect 5 = Neutral effect 10 = Very powerful effect	1 Sell to new customers	2 Sell more in each transaction	3 Persuade existing customers to return to your store more often	4 Improve margin by cutting overheads and improving sales quality
1 Joint activity	7	3	1	8
2 Displays in empty stores	5	0	5	8
3 Sponsorship and community events	4	0	10	4
4 Ads in changing rooms	0	10	6	6
5 Children's competitions	0	5	7	5
6 Tip sheets	8	6	8	9

7 Loyalty programs	0	5	10	3
8 Customer-get-customer	8	5	6	5
9 Buy one, get one free	8	7	10	2
10 Sampler clubs	1	5	10	7
11 Percentage off	6	7	6	3
12 Special nights	6	7	7	5
13 Surveys	6	0	8	6
14 Celebrity visit	10	0 or 10*	8	2
15 Book signings	8	0 or 10*	8	8
16 Lunch at the store	7	0	8	5
17 Seminars and "how-to" events	8	10	10	6
18 Meeting place	7	0	8	6
19 Charity giving	6	0	6	3
20 Local radio outside broadcasts	6	0	6	8
21 Banded product	8	5	8	7
22 Discount off future purchase	7	7	10	5
23 Gift certificate promotions	8	5	10	5
24 Buy now, pay later	7	5	7	4
25 Interest-free credit	8	6	8	5
26 Store card	2	8	7	10
27 Time-limited	10	4	4	1
28 Bargains	10	10	10	5

*   *A celebrity or author who is expert in the same field as the store can lead customers into buying all sorts of extras to go with a base purchase. However, a non-related one can't!*

Promotions planner

Putting together a promotions planner is simple but essential—you need to know when you're doing things and more importantly why you're doing them.

1   Start with 12 sheets of A4, one for each month of the year.

2   Write in all the things you can predict will be happening, for example a January Sale.

3 Then write down all the predictable quiet times for your business—summer vacations might be one.

4 Then write in all the predictable mad times such as Christmas.

5 Add any product launches that you know of.

6 Write in any major events that could offer some good promotion links, the Olympics or a blockbuster movie perhaps.

7 Now you will have a good idea where you have either dead zones to fill or crazy times to either avoid or strengthen, and you can see where some themed promotions might work well.

Choosing the right promotions is an art, but this information can really help you. For example, if your business is quiet during August because of summer vacations and most people being away, it might be sensible then to run promotions that maximize transaction values—pull more cash in from the few customers you do have at that time.

You can easily use a form of these planners to impress your potential new bosses at interviews too.

CHAPTER TWELVE

Marketing for real people

Tell me what it is, why I'd want one, and how to get it. That's all I give a damn about. If you can do that in a humorous, dramatic, or otherwise attention-grabbing way then, fine, knock yourself out. Please don't talk to me in Latin, use obtuse images, or hit me with stuff that goes way over my head because I just don't care enough about you or your product to bother trying to understand your clever rubbish.

In that one paragraph, you have all the rules of advertising you will ever need. Be clear, tell people what the benefit to them is, and then make it very easy for them to buy from you. Ad agencies argue that advertising is about building brands too. There is truth in this but, frankly, brand is built more powerfully by your shop, your people in it, and your store culture. Slick eye-candy advertising is simply not important.

Basic brands such as easyJet and Poundland tell you what they are for, why you would want to use them, and how to do business with them. Both those brands are sales heroes. Both are never going to win awards for the glossiness of their advertising. On the other hand, IKEA and Sainsbury's do the same thing but with a bigger budget, and arguably greater creative finesse, but to the same effect.

Advertising made simple

Media commentator Charlie Brooker wrote in his *Guardian* blog:

Marketing is the art of associating products with ideas to bamboozle consumers. People in marketing often talk about the "personality" of a given product. A biscuit might be "reassuring and sensual"; a brand of shoe may exhibit "anarchic yet inquisitive" tendencies. Marketers have built their worldview on such thinking, despite it being precisely the sort of babble a madman might come up with following years alone in an isolated cottage, during which time he falls in love with a fork and decides the lightbulbs are conspiring against him.

And, of course, he's right.

Beauty has its place

There is space for the beautiful—those breathtaking ads that force their way into your awareness. But these are very much the exception that rather proves the rule: You remember these because they are exceptional. Orange, the mobile phone network, has built a hugely successful brand without ever showing a picture of a telephone in its advertising (there was one, once, but Motorola was paying and forced the issue, but even then the phone featured was only shown as an x-ray image). You might think this goes against the simple doctrine I've outlined here. It doesn't. Orange's ads always tell you what they are for (mobile communications), they always focus on one clearly defined benefit at a time (say the joy of swapping pictures on a mobile), and then they put a great big phone number up on screen and suggest interested shoppers might like to call that to become an Orange customer.

Marketing things to make and do

Marketing is not a mythical black art; it is nothing more, or less, than a common sense framework: A framework into which ads and promotions can be fitted. Marketing theory is actually very simple. The skill, especially in the case of retail, is not in cleverly executing the practice of marketing but rather it is in trusting your gut feel to keep things simple. Marketing is about understanding who your customers are, where they can be found, what they want, and how much they will pay to satisfy those wants. That's really kind of it.

This sets up a series of questions. Who are we selling to? How do we tell them about our product? What will they pay for it? Notice how these questions form a chain? The answer to the first informs the second which in turn sets up the third. Answering these questions can help you to make better decisions on promotions and on advertising.

Questions chain

1   Who wants to shop at a store like mine?
2   What is it they like about us?
3   Which products excite them?
4   What promotions do they like?
5   Where can I find these people?
6   What should I tell them?

You might want to go through these questions in a team meeting. Try to cover four or five main customer types separately. Each customer type looked at will create a slightly different thread. Use what you learn to select target audiences and to select the promotions you would like to put before them. The following pages list some of your options for reaching those audiences.

Reaching customers—using recent technology

So you've worked out what you want to say and to whom; the next step is to choose your medium, or mix of media to reach them. The web has become an incredibly cost-effective option—sometimes costing you little more than time. You need to exploit these online communication options fully. So let's start with those:

Facebook

Get a company page set-up, use it to talk about the store, great products, promotions, and anything else that you think your customers will be interested in but that is also relevant to what you sell. Make the page look good, research it by looking at pages of retail businesses you know and respect—look at your own Facebook friends and take note of the company pages they've "liked."

Be prepared to take feedback directly on the page; it might hurt when that feedback is negative but it's important. The great thing about gathering feedback through Facebook and Twitter is that you tend to hear about problems early and so you have an early opportunity to solve them—and to show publicly that you have listened and dealt with an issue.

Twitter

Twitter can be daunting to the uninitiated—it looks like an absolute word-storm, but if thousands of other people can work it out, so can you. The best way to learn Twitter is to set up a personal account for yourself and, well, use it for a bit. Get to know the foibles and etiquette that way, without risking the store's reputation.

Once you're comfortable, set up an account for the store. Look at other popular retail brands on Twitter and see if you can work out what links them. You'll find the great ones tend to have a character to them: They transcend bland corporatism and feature an interesting mix of celebration of great product, news, comments, and tips.

Foursquare

This is one of the leaders in what are called "location-aware social games." It's similar in some ways to the "places" feature on Facebook but is much more flexible. In short: Members use their smartphones to tag whatever location they are in at the actual time they are in it. So a customer can be standing in your store and use Foursquare to tell all their friends they're there. Why would anyone bother to do that? It's a good question—tools such as Foursquare might fail to persist but, so far, investors and users are backing them heavily. What it enables is for individual stores to add their details and reward members for visiting the store: You can link promotions and all sorts to your site. It's free to do and Wetherspoons and Domino's have been among the first in the UK to realize the commercial potential.

Amazon and eBay

For most store types, even if you have your own transactional website, it's well worth also selling through Amazon Marketplace and eBay Stores. Both sites have astonishing reach and it doesn't require a great deal of effort to list your kit on their sites.

Smartphone and Tablet apps

Bit more involved this one, in terms of both cost and commitment; but for many stores, a smartphone app is a winner—it offers the opportunity to become integrated into customers" regular routines, which is so valuable. If you think it's worth doing then find yourself an expert—there are a number of app-developer matchmaking sites on the web.

YouTube/Vimeo

Make videos of staff celebrating product. Honest reviews, useful close-ups, relevant trivia—link to them from your website and Facebook page. Easy to do, customers love them, and they help build your character. Works best if the customer is then able to buy the featured product from you online but still worth doing if they can't.

Your own website

Now, if you're an Internet store then of course you've got this covered. But as I said at the start of the book, the disciplines of retail extend to whatever channel you sell through, and if you're a bricks-and-mortar store then you almost certainly need a transactional website too—one that represents you well and that gives customers another way in which to do business with you. Don't take this lightly—it's not good enough to post a half-assed webpage written by your weird cousin Tim. You must consider how the site reflects on your business: You need to think about how to get stock and POS systems working with the site and you need to think about how you are going to fulfill orders. None of these are trivial concerns. The same care and investment you made on your physical shop needs to be clear in your website too.

Case study 12.1 Smart Retail: ASOS takes it on the chin

ASOS.com is a brilliant retailer using the best of technology to stay crested right on top of the fashion waves. They also use great online tools to communicate with and learn from their customers; www.asosreviews.com is astonishingly clever: It aggregates ASOS mentions on Twitter and YouTube ▶

and allocates a "happy" or "sad" to the Tweets (yeah, that's what individual messages on Twitter are called, I know, I know)—those happies and sads are then used to generate a dynamic meter at the top of the page showing how happy, or otherwise, ASOS customers are. The feedback isn't costing ASOS much more than the cost of maintaining the website and it gives them immediate insight into how customers feel about them.

Reaching customers—traditional methods
Radio

Radio is a great medium. It's very cost-effective and you can paint any image you want with words. Often big and bold words work best. Plenty of stations will help you to create your ad. Each station will also be able to give you profiles of their listeners for each of their shows. This means you can choose to advertise only on those stations, and only during those shows, listened to by people who might actually want to shop with you. There are also lots of resources available for do-it-yourself radio advertisers, and that helps makes the medium very attractive.

The Radio Advertising Bureau exists "to guide national advertisers and their agencies toward effective advertising on Commercial Radio." They won't be able to advise you directly but their website is a fantastic mine of resources. Click on the truly heroic radio advert archive; all the inspiration you could ever want is there. The RAB's web address is www.rab.co.uk.

TV

TV is undoubtedly a powerful advertising channel, but it's expensive and it suffers a tendency to be somewhat scattergun in effect. Unless you can afford to advertise on TV lots then it's unlikely that you will reach enough of your potential customers to make this medium pay. The Advertising Association, www.adassoc.org.uk, has some useful research on its site that you might want to take a look at if you're considering TV. The channels themselves do offer advice and assistance to smaller advertisers, so it is worth asking about those services. Ask too about related discounted advertising packages.

Print

Clear bold messages work best, and buy the largest portrait spot you can afford. Don't do national if you are local. Don't be seduced by glamorous graphics. A bold typographical treatment highlighting a great promotion accompanied by a shot of your product is more effective. And the old maxim of "less is more" absolutely applies.

Posters

Traditional large-format posters can act like a second storefront, but they are expensive. These days the sites available for placing an ad are almost without limit: everything from posters in bar bathrooms to the handles of gas pumps. JCDecaux is the largest independent outdoor media owner in the UK and worth talking to if you are interested in exploring posters. Their web address is www.jcdecaux.co.uk.

Catalogs

A catalog can be a single flyer or a 32-page color extravaganza. Never underestimate the power of catalogs. They provide you with huge scope to tell people about your fantastic deals and at the same time talk about why your store is a nice place to visit and to do business with. George Whalin, one of America's most effective retail consultants, suggests that "if you have one item and just one page, that's a catalog, start from there and build it over time."

Never underestimate the power of catalogs.

Catalogs are exciting because there is so much you can do with them. You can hand them out as flyers, you can put them into the local free papers, you can mail them to your customer database, and you can give them out to visitors to your store.

Consider how you might distribute your catalog. Piles in the store are fine; a stand outside is better. Having a colleague hand them out in the parking lot or up and down the street is always worth doing. Paying a delivery person to distribute catalogs door-to-door is useful too. Of course, this is also dependent on the type of catalog you have gone for. If yours is thick, heavy, and expensive then distribution will have to be more limited. Similarly, if you know that your customer falls into a very narrow interest group then you should consider distributing your catalog directly to them—a baby goods store might want to have its catalog in the waiting area of the local maternity ward for example.

Easy ABC database marketing

Every store can, and must, build a customer database. Used sensibly they drive customers into your store like no other advertising tool can. You don't need complex software to run them: Any database program such as Microsoft's Access will do. You can even get by fine using just the contacts bit of the free program Outlook Express (again available from Microsoft) or on Google Mail. A card index will suffice in high-ticket selling situations where you are servicing a small number of prospect customers.

The best email marketing
How to do email database marketing really well

1   Always get permission; customers hate email spam and junk mail—it irritates them. They respond much better to expected messages, so long as these are relevant.

2   Make sure you actually have something to say, for example:

▶   Exclusive offer

▶   Hard-to-get item here in stock now

▶   End-of-line special bargain

▶   One-off event

▶   Exciting new line due in on date x

3   Start the email with all your headings—just titles with no additional body text, for example:

▶   Buy-one-get-one-free on all paperback fiction this weekend only

▶   New Dan Brown arrives in-store here on June 11—reserve your copy now

▶   David Beckham here signing his new autobiography on July 1

4   Remember: Time limits on offers always help to drive customers into action.

5 Then in the body of the email, below these headlines, you can expand on each subject. Try to keep words to a minimum: Just tell the story and then get out.

▶ Buy one-get-one-free on all paperback fiction this weekend only.

▶ Choose any two from our huge range of great titles and you get the cheapest free; that includes all of our current best-sellers as well as the full selection of classic fiction. Saturday and Sunday only—we're looking forward to seeing you!

6 Remember: Close with details of your store including telephone numbers and opening times.

7 Sign it! Customers appreciate a personal touch.

8 Remember the rules: "Tell me what it is, tell me why I might want one, tell me how to get it."

The Data Protection Act

If you are going to hold customers" data in a database, you must comply with the Data Protection Act 1998. Most retailers have notified that they wish to be registered under the Act. If you have done so, you are likely to be entitled to also use the data you hold for database marketing purposes. You must check though before moving on. If you are in a chain-store branch, the company may well have notified too but it can be tricky to find out. If you are lucky, the marketing team will find out for you and will help you with the small number of compliance issues involved. If you are less lucky and the marketing team gets all sloppy, then it may be worth considering notifying in the name of your individual store instead. Lots of clear advice on the whole process can be found at www.dataprotection.gov.uk/dpr/dpdoc.nsf.

One of the key aspects of the Data Protection Act is permission. When you ask for someone's details, you must tell them that you will be holding these details in a database. You must also get their permission to send them things. Check on the www.dataprotection.gov.uk site for the latest advice on what to say and how to say it. Getting permission is good practice anyway—there is little point in taking someone's address only to send them things they don't want to see.

Postcards

Email is the nice, easy, and cheap way to begin database marketing. There is an excellent print alternative, though, that is still cost-effective, espe-

Email is the nice, easy, and cheap way to begin database marketing.

cially as a tool for announcing big promotions or sales or as invites to store events. Stores in the U.S. use postcard marketing campaigns very effectively.

The usual format is a large postcard where one side is given over to a full-color image and the other side is split into two halves. One of those halves is a space to put an address label and a stamp. The other half will then usually carry a coupon of some sort.

Local printers are plentiful, so get three price quotes and ask to see samples. Get a fixed-cost quote and some examples. Make sure you and the printer both understand exactly what it is that you want. Short print runs are ideal as this lets you over time send lots of different messages to individual targeted groups of customers.

Selecting prospects to send your cards to needs a bit of thought. You want to avoid wastage and to maximize your chances of success. All current and recent customers who could conceivably need to visit you again should be targeted. Think carefully, though: Writing to someone who bought a sofa from you last week to tell them you are offering 10% off sofas this week is always going to be a bad idea.

Think about your customers; do groups of them have particular things in common? Do you find yourself selling to people who all live in certain areas of town? Are your products related to their hobbies, or to their work? Are there any age groups that you seem to attract disproportionately? Looking at these factors will help you to identify other groups of people who are not your customers yet who are very much like your existing ones. These prospect groups are almost certainly worth talking to, and a postcard offer might just do the trick.

Case study 12.2 Smart Retail: Postcards and the 20%

"Whenever we run a campaign and promote it using postcards, our sales increase by 20%." Andrea Cohen runs young retail business number 35, based in London (see p. 146). She's been successfully trading two stores for some time now and is all set for expanding the brand as a chain. Like a lot of new retailers, number 35 began life located slightly off-pitch, in this case a secondary street off Highgate's main shopping area. That meant the store had to work harder to gain a foothold in customers" minds. Number 35 sells a unique product, its own collection of women's clothes tailored to modern shapes—apparently women are that bit more curved in today than they were when most clothes brands cut their patterns. The clothes are great and customer feedback is stunning—for some, number 35's clothes are the answer to a heart-felt prayer. See for yourself at www.no35.co.uk.

The other challenge Andrea has is that these are clothes made to fit the real shape of modern women—some customers confuse that with "outsize" when actually the range focuses on sizes 8 to 16. So, normal sizes but cut to fit really well. It's a message that needs that tiny bit of explanation and postcard promotions fit the bill nicely. So Andrea's technique has been to create a year's worth of promotions and events and then to drop postcards, via a local newspaper, to support them. The effect is interesting—although often the promotional items themselves only sell in low numbers, reminding customers that the store exists and telling them what the big idea is has the effect of raising overall revenue significantly after each campaign.

Andrea and the first number 35 store.
Source: Andrea Cohen

Keeping track—measurement

Any direct activity needs to be made measurable. You can do this easily by adding coded coupons to printed materials, and by asking email customers to quote a reference code when they come in. It doesn't matter if the customer cannot remember the code, just that they tell you they want to take advantage of an offer you emailed to them.

Set up a basic Microsoft Excel spreadsheet to make tracking easy. Literally, just a few columns for the dates and then a few rows for the various promotions you are running. Then record the number of people responding, the total value of their purchases, and the margin earned on each transaction. At the end of each week, work out the total profit accounted for by your promotions. Then deduct from that the cost of the activity you ran. So long as you capture every relevant sale, then this is a crude but perfectly acceptable way to track how well each promotion is working for you.

You also need to take account of the discounts you gave to normal customers: People who would have bought from you regardless of the promotion. That is quite tricky and will often be down to your instinctive judgement. All the same, it is important because this number helps you to realistically appraise returns from your efforts.

PART FOUR—**STORE**

Make it brilliant and they will spend.

**That's a supermarket! Austria's MPREIS chain uses hot archi-
tects to design every store—each is then unique. They use the
very fabric of the store to differentiate their business.**
Source: MPREIS/Thomas Jantscher

The Fundamentals

When customers wander around your store, or look into its windows, they are subconsciously demanding "INSPIRE ME! MAKE ME WANT TO LOOK AT SOMETHING!" If there is a trick to retailing, it's in understanding how to manage that demand to your advantage. The principal tools you have to do that with are:

▶ Your external communications

▶ Windows

▶ Use of retail theater

▶ Discovery

Those tools will be wielded passively by the store and actively by you and the team. I'm going to talk about discovery first because it both informs everything else but also because it's the one of those four that was most likely to have made you say "you what?" Let's turn a bit of jargon into some practical good stuff then ...

CHAPTER THIRTEEN

Discovery!

All shopping is about discovery. Even the customer who is certain they just want Heinz tomato ketchup week-in and week-out is disruptable by a good promotion or interesting new alternative—and they delight in it, even if that new discovery turns out to be disappointing. The point at which discovery is made may shift, but no shopping trip is ever made without it. Our role as retailers is to work out how to make discovery work for us to generate a sale.

Point of discovery

Sometimes the discovery will be made before leaving the house: Research having been done online, in magazines, and among friends. That certainly applies to a more significant degree on big-ticket items but even then, having spent years watching actual customer behavior in-store, I suspect not as often as we might assume. Indeed, McKinsey & Company conducted research in 2010 that suggests 40% of customers who leave home knowing what they want, having extensively researched it and used all the tools online to help with that, are still "open to persuasion" once they arrive at the store.

Discovery makes people touch things. Make a customer say "wow" in your store and you've got a sale. Discovery is not just about showing customers surprising things; it is the complete process of helping to guide them to the highlights of your range, to the great promotions, to using great service to lead customers to the right choices and to structuring whole formats to provide moments of discovery throughout the customer journey.

Make a customer say "wow" in your store and you've got a sale.

If you're managing a store within a chain, it's well worth picking up the principles of discovery and making them squeeze your store's merchandising to the limits. Try stuff and communicate back everything that works—use this as an opportunity to influence the direction of the business and to raise your personal profile. If, dear reader, you're one of those lucky people in a position to create, adapt, or relaunch a format then I urge you to put discovery at the center of your thinking. Doing so will increase footfall, increase conversion, and help your team to maximize average transaction values.

Benefits of building formats around discovery
Footfall

A reputation as a store that can meet customers" subconscious desire for discovery will drive your footfall. Customers tend to visit stores that meet their needs—a need for inspiration, surprise, and ideas is satisfied in a store that has built discovery into its format and merchandising. At its simplest, it's about making yours a store that people out on a shopping trip feel like they want to drop into "just because."

Conversion rate

This is a no-brainer: If you can actively get more of the best parts of your range into the minds and hands of customers as they browse your store then the more often you will convert those browsers into buyers.

Average transaction value

Discovery is also about the total sale—everything a customer might need to get the best out of their purchase. So, that might be accessories with clothes, insurance with a phone, sauces with the pasta. It's also about creating such a credible service-position that your people are better able to give customers the right advice on a total package—especially important in big-ticket situations.

Linking it all together

This is all good simple stuff still—the only hard part of all this is in ensuring that there is consistency along through your Big Idea, mission, values, and into the way in which you tackle discovery. It's a little bit chicken-and-egg, but faced with a blank sheet of paper, I would be making sure that my Big Idea was something that can be delivered with the techniques of discovery. Mission and values, what the business exists to do, and the spirit in which it does it should then nicely slot into that.

The different types of discovery

There are broadly four approaches to tackling discovery: promotion-led, service-led, product-led, and format-led. A small handful of retailers—Lush, Pret A Manger, and Stew Leonard's (see later) included—take advantage of discovery across all four approaches and others combine two, sometimes three. Where I've listed a retailer as a great exponent of a particular approach, it's because that's the one that's at the heart of what they do best.

Traditional promotion-led discovery

This is the most common approach, and if you're able to offer great deals, it's very powerful. The availability of those deals is only half the story

Be a kid again—get enthused by discovery.
Source: Koworld

though—really high-quality merchandising is the critical component: getting your deals, and the benefits of them, into customers" faces.

Toolkit

- ▶ Creative promotions
- ▶ Variety of promotions
- ▶ A near-guarantee that there will be a deal for every customer, every time
- ▶ Consistent low prices on core products
- ▶ A retail type that encourages regular revisit
- ▶ Celebration of the offers by putting them in good locations and regular inclusion of the "good stuff"
- ▶ Store layout that includes plenty of hot spots
- ▶ Planned customer journey that leads visitors between those hot spots

Tesco (UK)

The international blueprint for promotion-led discovery: Go walk their floor as an observer and learn how to select, place, and promote offers brilliantly.

Aldi (Germany)

While I'm not entirely keen on the management structures within Aldi stores (managers have very little say in the basic running of their stores), it is understandable and contributes to an interesting twist on the discount supermarket. Aldi aren't just about being cheap—an important component in the store's reputation is the quality of product it sells, even if that product is a special buy and discounted down to the ground. By restricting the variety of options per line (fewer suppliers, far fewer lines overall, and so much larger product orders and potential for significant discounts as a result), standardizing everything to within an inch of its life, spending less on fixtures, and requiring less space than a traditional supermarket they carve themselves a price-led position relative to those supermarkets. But by maintaining product quality, they also then differentiate themselves from the Lidls and Nettos and are able to attract more middle-class spend.

B&Q (UK)

Always good at promotional deals but what puts them into this premier division of promotion-led discovery is their approach to pricing core project items. Let's take decking—the deck planks themselves are almost priced to give way, a few pounds only for each 3m length: A wandering customer will do their initial value calculation—the one done in your head when you've actually come in for something else—based on the cost of the decking planks alone. That makes the cost of the project appear to be very low. It is only then when adding the cost of frame timbers, posts, screws, joints, and finishes that the true project cost emerges. By this point, it's a bit academic because you've already pictured yourself out on the deck enjoying a summer barbecue.

Boots (UK)

Poor old Boots comes in for a lot of stick but I believe it's a fantastic retailer. Boots is really a dreary old drug store, yet customers like to drop in for treats, bargains, and gifts—that's a stunning leap out from their core purpose. One of the things Boots does really well, and that's helped them to make that profitable leap, is promotions—they practically own the concept of three-for-two offers and are very good at communicating these offers, displaying them and refreshing them.

Service-led discovery

This is all about using your people to provide customers with a fantastic discovery experience. We're talking motivated, well-trained, professional teams encouraged to dedicate themselves to providing the best honest advice, suggestions, and after-sales service. Keys to achieving this are all written up in the "Team" section of this book—go do that stuff. Your customers will love you for it—love you with their wallets.

Toolkit

▶ Make it clear that you trust your team with your customers, that your number one priority is the satisfaction of both.

▶ Treat your people with respect.

▶ Offer them great training and lots of it.

▶ Allow and enable your people to experience the products you sell: Give them big staff discounts and operate loan programs for new products.

▶ Get your people involved in the supply chain: Allow them to see how things are sourced and made—doing so will help them to enthuse about your products and, more importantly, to identify what makes your stuff great.

▶ Structure your reward program such that it is biased toward customer satisfaction and away from sales volumes.

▶ Put in place a recognition program and use it to say "thank you" each and every time you see your people go the extra mile for customers.

▶ Value knowledge highly but also encourage your team to always be open-minded and make sure they understand that every customer has their own set of needs.

▶ Stress the value of listening to what customers tell us they need and show how this is more important than telling customers what we assume they should have.

The Container Store (U.S.)

They are brilliant at this. The Container Store provides phenomenal levels of training and wonderful employment experiences and works incredibly hard to build stable customer-focused teams. The result is a business that punches well above its weight and that enjoys a near fanatical level of customer support. One of my favorite retailers anywhere in the world. They provide an average of 210 hours/year staff training, great staff discounts, and have featured in *Fortune*'s 100 Best Places to Work in America list for 11 years straight.

Carphone Warehouse (UK)

I get a bit of stick for holding up CPW as an example of great retailing so often, but I'm not going to apologize for that. When a retailer is this good, and for all the right reasons, then they need to be singled out. CPW is all about service-led discovery: Customers walk into these stores often with nothing more than the notion that they want a new mobile phone. They do so, overwhelmingly, with the prior knowledge that the CPW assistant will honestly, and accurately, discover the right answers to that vague need.

John Lewis Partnership (UK)

A byword for honesty, quality, and great customer care in the UK. Customers are drawn to John Lewis because they feel sure that the team there will help them to discover the right stuff for them. JLP has been especially good at doing this in high-ticket electronics and computing—areas perhaps not traditionally associated with the store but that, nonetheless, customers feel good about letting John Lewis guide them through.

Product-led discovery

Where the product is the star: Innovation, fashion, trends, great iconic design are the critical factors in stores where the product leads discovery. So, we're talking about the kinds of stores that are great at buying and merchandising and at refreshing the ranges. But it's more than that—it's critical that the top team in this sort of store have an innate understanding of the principles and power of design and that they have a sense for the zeitgeist among their target customer groups. A lot of expensive single-store businesses start up as retail businesses in this category and an awful lot of them fail—they fail because the owners mistake "knowing what I like" with "knowing what customers want." When done right, though, the approach can be incredibly successful—the very best fashion and furnishings stores are great examples of product-led discovery shops.

Toolkit

▶ It's all about your buying: Spotting exceptional products at the right price points.

▶ Hang on, maybe it's all about your merchandising: Showing off those products in inspirational settings?

▶ Study all the sources of information on trends you can find: Subscribe to trade-specific designers" magazines such as *Frame* and *Creative Design*.

▶ Watch what goes on in competitors" stores very closely for clues on trends.

▶ Talk to customers, get feedback all the time.

▶ Ask customers what's hot, encourage them to make recommendations on new finds and new directions.

▶ Investigate design leads.

▶ Ensure key products are given room to breathe and are displayed to their absolute best.

▶ Be prepared to drop poor-performing lines early (or at least to change emphasis if you can).

▶ Refresh ranges often but show respect for important classic lines too.

▶ Do not presume to dictate taste but do try hard to influence it.

ASOS (UK)

The store launched in 2000 with the name "As Seen On Screen"—the Big Idea was to sell clothes seen on celebs and actors on TV and in the movies. A great niche proposition. The management team there quickly outgrew that space as they discovered that they were good at tracking screen-seen stuff but even better at understanding and stocking up-to-date fashions in general. That awesome instinct for fashion, and a focused concentration on the 16–34 age range, has driven product-led discovery and created a store that customers love to regularly check out.

Habitat (UK)

It's in a right old state at the moment, but there are lessons from Habitat's history that are worth looking at here. From Sir Terence Conran's early days creating the business, Habitat was at the forefront of shaping British living. Habitat sold the duvet to a country raised under scratchy sheets and they did it by explaining to us that the duvet represented freedom from domestic chores. They made every 1980s kitchen complete by selling each and every last man, woman, and child on the planet a bright red, yellow, blue or green teapot; they helped my Mom and Dad feel comfortable enough to throw dinner parties by suggesting that a chicken brick, or a pressure cooker, was the secret to successful entertaining. Mom and Dad divorced in 1988, so I'm blaming Habitat for that too.

Zara (Spain)

Zara is built on an incredibly efficient supply chain that enables it to bring new items into stores twice a week, every week. That's an astonishing commitment to product-led discovery—they lead the fashion retail industry on logistics and are able to take an idea from initial design to retail rail faster than anybody else. It's obvious to see why customers might react positively to such fast change and ever-shifting variety.

Top Shop (UK)

No other fashion store anywhere in the world is as good as Top Shop currently is at product-led discovery. No young British woman, and no hip visitor to the UK, leaves Top Shop out of their shopping trip. The sheer weight of fantastic, right-on-the-money fashion that blitzes through the store and into customers' wardrobes is truly mind-boggling. As my earlier case study on them suggests, this is almost entirely down to Top Shop's commitment to stocking only stuff they love. Everything they sell works or it's dropped fast, ranges are refreshed at speed, one-offs come in and go out (and onto eBay) at the blink of an eye, and even the celebs like to say they've been in and raided Top Shop. The business is all about making customers feel the urge to come in as often as possible in a bid to discover the best new stuff before anyone else does.

Format-led discovery

There are a number of retailers who have based their entire Big Idea and format around discovery and paths to discovery. These are the stores you find full of handwritten notices recommending products. They are the ones in which you see little notes to you, the customer, all over the place that connect you with the products. Everything in the store is about making sure that you are made aware of how brilliant product X will be for you, how you will feel, what a difference this thing will make to your health, well-being, or lifestyle. That sounds a bit "ad-man" written down. It's worth saying that in order to properly convince the format must be honest, credible, and authentic too. Oh, and this is important: Format-led discovery only works if there is service-led discovery in place too.

Toolkit

▶ Create an authentic voice for the brand.

▶ Use your values to ensure that voice properly represents your Big Idea and mission.

▶ Create a compelling conversation throughout the customer journey: Make use of space on product, bags, shelf-edge, in changing rooms, on product cartons, walls, bags, editorial, at the cash register, and so on.

▶ Provide honest advice, from written communications through to staff advice.

▶ Celebrate the great products: Be enthusiastic, explain to customers why you think item X is so great.

▶ Constantly refresh displays.

▶ Get customers involved with recommendations.

▶ Make good use of customer advocacy: Make it easy for customers to tell others about your store and range.

▶ Remember that it's the conversation that's important.

▶ Make good use of seasonal and "occasion" events.

Apple Store (U.S.)

These iconic retail bases for Apple's products are entirely about discovery. They are built, from the ground up, around the notion of non-Apple people discovering that Apple meets their needs better and of dedicated Apple users discovering more that they can do with their Apple products. So you have every single part of the Apple range, in quantity, out on the shop-floor set up so customers can touch them, play with them, have fun with them, and discover new things with them. Then the Apple Genius team, extremely well-trained customer advisors, make themselves easily available to give advice, recommendations and solutions. In the early days, I wondered if the Apple Stores would turn out to be heavily subsidized brand promotion rather than profitable stores; the opposite is true—the stores are very profitable as well as being stunningly successful discovery zones for loyal and new Apple customers alike.

Target (U.S.)

The team here recognized that in order to beat Kmart and to avoid a Wal-Mart smothering, they would need to offer something different within the variety-store format—and they chose discovery. They did that by building the entire store around innovative displays, by bringing in young and hot designers, through a perfect collaboration with Martha Stewart, and by creating a much friendlier and more open atmosphere than is usual in this type of store. Indeed, Wal-Mart has even been forced into creating a sub-format to tackle Target on Target's ground: These slightly more-upmarket Wal-Marts drop the McDonald's narrow aisles and guns and replace them with better-quality fixtures, more space, and independent café concessions.

Pret A Manger (UK)

These sandwich shops do authentic conversation better than any other retailer in the world. Should you find yourself reading this book while sitting at one of Pret's stainless-steel counters, you would find that the coffee cup you're drinking from has a note on it that explains how Pret's coffee has come to taste as good as it does. That cup would explain too how Pret supports the grower of the beans your coffee was made from. You might then dab the corners of your mouth with a Pret napkin that tells you it's made from unbleached, recycled fibers and that explains why that's a good thing. This conversation Pret A Manger has with its customers is powerful and is about helping customers to discover a lunchtime option that meets a perceived deeper set of needs. There's a lot of research evidence which proves that human beings' sense of taste is affected by contextual information—telling somebody that they should expect to enjoy their sandwich more because it is fresh increases the likelihood that they will enjoy it more. You can use that in lots of ways in retail—we're generally really bad at communicating emotional or sensual information so directly to our customers.

Lush (UK)

The store you smell before you see it has format-led discovery pretty much sewn up. Everywhere you look there are "handwritten" (actually printed but made to look handwritten) signs full of humor and passion telling you why they love the stuff they love. Lush's discovery positioning was born out of a Big Idea that was genuinely new: to create cosmetics from pure fruit and vegetable ingredients with no link, at any stage, to animal testing. Instead of being terribly po-faced about that positioning, the team behind Lush chose instead to have fun. Stores are merchandised in a unique way that sits somewhere between authentic French market-stall, English jumble sale, and display stand at an expo—I like it a lot, it's all really easy for customers and staff to interact with the product and with each other.

Urban Outfitters (U.S.)

You'll notice that I categorize most fashion stores in the product-led discovery category. Urban Outfitters make the jump because of the innovative way they have constructed their display systems, the credible addition of non-clothes ranges and the considered inclusion of branded ranges. All displays at Urban Outfitters are mix-and-match—tables, shelves, and rails can be easily combined, moved and re-merchandised. This makes it easy for the team to constantly refresh the store and to use a form of convection to bring different items to the surface before allowing these to settle back into main stock as new items get pulled to the surface.

Case study 13.1 Exceptionally Smart Retail: Stew's not mad ...

Stew Leonard's is barking. Often literally. Oh, and it's baa'ing, moo'ing, and clucking too, much of the time. Stew's is a chain of just four stores in north-east USA that together take $300,000,000 a year. They turn nearly ▶

four thousand dollars per square foot and that achieves revenue-per-employee above $150,000. Staggering, stunning, mind-blowing numbers.

And what is Stew Leonard's?

A dairy store.

Yep. They sell a limited selection of 1,000 dairy and dairy-related products—albeit within massive mega-sites. Up to 125,000 customers each week. Those numbers are just unreal.

And although I suspect current boss Stew Leonard Jr. wouldn't call it by this name, discovery is what sits at the heart of the amazing performance of this business. The entire format is built around discovery: loads to see and do and a massive single aisle that snakes customers past every last part of the massive store. Promotion-led discovery is there in spades, and in massive volume. Product-led discovery too is important with, in particular, what they claim to be the freshest milk in North America—which they bottle on-site in a glassed-in lab visible to all customers. Service-led promotion is incredibly important too: the employment experience at Stew Leonard's is of a very high standard (and regularly recognized as such in *Fortune Magazine*'s "100 Best Companies to Work For" annual list).

The customer is king here but only because the staff are allowed to make it so. "You can't have a great place to shop, without first making it a great place to work"—that's a slogan you'll see written up in the store, but it's more than words—the management team deliver on that too.

Stew Leonard's give every employee a real say in how to best service customer needs. If an employee thinks that doing X is good for the one customer in front of them, they will get on and do it. If they think Y is good for all customers then they will suggest the business gets on and does that too. There is a great story Stew Jr. tells that illustrates this in action. He calls it the tuna fish story: "I unwrap one of our tuna fish sandwiches, and this package of mayonnaise rolls out. I figure the sandwich has enough mayo already. So I call Bill Hollis, my deli manager, and tell him 'get rid of the extra mayo, it's expensive.' So next week, I open a sandwich, the mayo rolls out again. I call Bill, and he says 'you gotta talk to Mary Ekstrand, she makes the sandwiches.' I call Mary, who says "Sorry, Stew, the customers want the extra mayo, so I'm packing it again.' You know my reaction? Bravo, Mary!"

Stew Jr. has a cheesy but perfect acronym that illustrates his management style nicely—STEW: Satisfy the customer; work together as a Team; strive for Excellence at everything you do; and get the customer to say WOW.

That "wow" thing is a foundation principle of all forms of discovery: It means customers have found stuff that meets that discovery need. The team have created what the *New York Times* calls "The Disneyland of Dairy Stores," and it is—banjo-playing robot dogs sing "Dixie," and animatronic milk cartons (The Farm Fresh Five) dance near a model cow that tells jokes when kids pull its bell. Staff dress as cows, ducks, chickens, and bananas while patroling the aisles, giving out free ice cream and helium balloons. Free food samples are everywhere and staff offer them accompanied by warm, genuine smiles. There are petting zoos, outdoor BBQs, beach grills, cafes, and singing broccoli and carrots. Shoppers don't just come here to buy a quart of milk—they come for the experience. An experience built on discovery.

Thing is—this store might feel like it's lots of things all just thrown together but that's not really true. This is a place built by its people—those 125,000 customers come along each week because they like the products; sure, they come for the atmosphere, definitely, but mostly I suspect they come because the human experience at Stew Leonard's makes them feel good. That it does so is down to the dedication, imagination, and vision not of just one man but of a whole motivated, passionate team.

14

The great big theater of shop

The Stew Leonard's case study featured some great big dripping chunks of retail theater—an idea that's so critical to creating great customer experiences. Theater. Hmm, we love a bit of Shakespeare and all that … I'm not talking about that sort of theater. Well, I am actually, but not in the same way: retail theater is about animating the store, making it live and breathe. Telling stories with color, sound, movement, and even smells and tastes.

"What for?" is the reasonable question. The answer is: Bringing the store to life brings your customers to life too. Your biggest challenge is to get customers to pick up stuff and interact with it and with staff—get that happening and you sell more things. If that interaction is done inside a great, animated, and exciting store, then you get the Stew Leonard effect: A humble dairy becomes a sales machine and customers love it.

When I talked about customer experiences in the customer service quality bit earlier, this is the part I was building up to—the part where everything you are and do comes to life.

Us, the moles, and the bats

We have a challenge in-store: Human sight is really, really poor when compared to most other mammals'—in particular, our low-resolution eyes coupled to our face-pattern-recognizing and motion-obsessed brains make seeing static things difficult. It is physiologically hard for people to pick out one thing from another if those things are static: like, say, cans of food on a fixture or a row of TVs on display or books packed in on shelves.

Let me put on the lab coat and explain: What we think we see is actually the image after it's been messed around with by our brain. Our brain applies two visual processes in particular that are great for survival of the species but pointless for retailing. The first relates to faces: Our big juicy brains are constantly looking to recognize faces so we can either defend ourselves from a competitive human or mate with a willing one. So aggressively does our brain look for faces that it'll make them out of almost anything: patterns in wallpaper, shapes made by shadows, a gravy stain on a shirt. This process is exactly why people report seeing the face of Michael Jackson in slices of toast or dead relatives in the shape of clouds. The more challenging process is the one that refuses to concentrate on static things and instead scans peripheral vision for movement, because in the past, bigger things were often trying to eat us and they tended to do so successfully by sneaking up without being noticed until it was too late.

Let's talk about that in a retail situation: You'll have experienced what I'm about to describe—we all have. You're standing in the soup aisle in a supermarket facing the hundreds of cans of soup. You want chicken noodle and you're staring and staring but you just can't see the one you want. And then, suddenly, "BANG!" you finally spot the can and it's been right in front of you all the time. You didn't see it at first because your brain was paying attention to somebody on your left moving something down off the shelf, to a shopping cart being pushed along to your right, and to a sign moving in the air-conditioning breeze above you. You found the chicken noodle in the end because your brain kicked in a different process called "reading," forcing you to read labels, which is slower than looking for pictures and patterns.

Movement

Applying one part of retail theater can solve these issues at a stroke—picking stuff up, moving it around attracts customers" attention. You pick up a can of soup and wave it about and suddenly it's the easiest thing in the world to see—everyone in that aisle can pick it out. Now, maybe that's not practical in Tesco, but it is most everywhere else. Let me give you an example and a case study.

Impulse cakes

The example is one you can observe for yourself and it involves the express line in a typical urban supermarket. If you're there and you see a member of staff re-stocking the racks of small cakes and treats that are usually stationed at the point where the line-guide turns ... watch what happens ... of the next ten people in the line, eight of them will at least pick up a cake and of those most will buy it. Then contrast that with the rest of the time when the fixture isn't being re-stocked: You'll see maybe one in ten customers picking up a cake. I'm not exaggerating these numbers—observe it for yourself and think about an area of your store that might be boosted by movement, by taking something out of stasis and giving it energy.

Case study 14.1 Smart Retail: Kinetically charged books

A client of ours, a chain of bookstores, made one small change that boosted sales by up to 20% per store. And it was such a tiny change too. They had asked us to find a way to schedule shelf-stocking so that it could be done away from customers—the logic being "get the book cart off the shop floor before we get busy." I asked them why this was a problem and they reckoned that it looked scruffy stocking shelves and that "as soon as you put something on the shelf, a customer will take it off again."

Now then, I hope you're ahead of me right now—that client was seeing it as an unprofessional irritation, but you're already seeing an opportunity, aren't you? What was happening is that the books, which when static are nothing more than shapes with colors on them, had been given a boost of kinetic energy and customers were drawn to them. So, instead, we created a routine in which books would be shelved at the busiest periods, and we told staff that they were welcome to take all day to do it, provided the delay was because they were having conversations about books with customers who were drawn to the movement. And they did exactly this.

We even did things like taking all the books off one table, putting them on the floor near a different table, then taking the books off the second table and putting them on the first, finishing the job by picking up the original books off the floor and putting them on the now-clear second table. Of ▶

course, we let the staff in on the gag—explaining that what looked like a nonsense job was actually generating movement and attracting customers. They loved it because it seemed to break a small barrier between them and customers—it seemed easier to start conversations as this process went on.

All of the above is retail theater: movement, visual interest. Go to a good hair salon and you'll find instinctive performers delivering theatrical experiences there: the smell of product, the noise of the music and the dryers, the performance of stylists cutting, the colors, the action. You'll find great theater at AllSaints (UK), Les Néréides (France), Lush (UK), McDonald's (U.S.), Bloomingdale's (U.S.), Printemps (France), Kiehl's (U.S.), and Bic Camera (Japan). You'll see it at great independents such as Rough Trade East (London, UK), Powell's City of Books (Portland, Oregon) and Robert Moy's Tuscan Pots (Oxford, UK—tiny store but the best indi-retailer I know, anywhere. Awesome place, go visit).

Case study 14.2 Smart Retail: Ceremonies

A neat way to introduce theater into your store is to break down everything you do into small "ceremonies"—little routines that create a bit of difference, done with a flourish. At brilliant hotel chain Malmaison, they pack these theatrical ceremonies into eveything. An example is seen in the way they deal with a dinner order for a glass of port: Instead of bringing you a glass of port, they bring a clean empty glass and their port decanter. Your glass is placed down and the port in poured there in front of you. It's a process that adds very little to the time it takes to serve a glass of port but it looks fantastic to the customer—the lovely liquid appetizingly pouring out, the gently pleasing glass-filling sound, and the rich color of a generously filled decanter.

Boutique French jewelry brand Les Néréides is hot right now and their London showcase store is always buzzing. It's a store in which lots of ceremonies add up to a deliciously satisfying customer experience. It starts with a visually reinforcing store layout: Everything is fresh, collections are given room to breathe, and staff are dressed in sweet summery clothes that match well with the design ethos of the jewelry. That's theater too—it's the equivalent of great set and costumes. As soon as customers interact with the habitually happy and approachable staff, the ceremonies kick in: Lots of drawers of product are removed and placed upon the counter, but in a set way so that only the items that are currently "in play" are visible. Ideas and suggestions are freely offered and they will ask customers for whom the purchase is to be made.

You'll see women buying for themselves given mirrors and encouraging comment, and you'll see assistants trying on necklaces to help men buying gifts for partners. It's incredibly human and involving. Then purchases are wrapped in paper and the paper sprayed with the house-scent, they are dropped into nicely designed gift bags that seem modern and classic all at the same time (much like the jewelry) and finally the bag is tied ostentatiously with a pretty bow. The whole process is full of ceremonies and it makes the experience feel very special indeed.

Fundamentals of retail theater

For our next journey into retail theater, we're going happily out onto the street—we'll maybe even learn about other parts of the puzzle too. That's because the best lesson on the fundamentals of retail you could ever have is to be found at traditional street markets. In particular, the fruit and vegetablee-table stalls on those markets. Right there is where you will see the most efficient, simple, and effective principles all in action—not because somebody has an MBA but instead because those principles have been passed down over the generations. From father to son, from mother to daughter—because they work.

Seriously, I can't recommend strongly enough that you go and quietly observe the dynamics of a busy street market. While you're there, take a look at these two.

A—Vocal promotion
B—Merchandising

A—Vocal promotion

Traders calling out to shoppers can be exhilarating to watch, especially when it's done well. What you can learn from listening to these calls (it's called "barking" apparently) is a sense of what really turns customers on. The lines shouted out have been passed down from trader to trader over generations. Traders still use them because they make customers react. Go beyond the old-time vocal theatricals and you can see some incredible promotional instinct at work. In particular, fruit and vegetable sellers do two things when they bark:

▶ They bark the promotions "two for one"

▶ But listen closely to the words they use when describing the produce—it's not just "cherry, strawberry, apples, oranges, pineapples." You'll hear "Sweet cherry!," "Lovely ripe strawberry!," "Get your crunchy fresh apples!," "Juicy golden pineapple!"

The adjectives—fresh, delicious, ripe, sweet, rosy-red, juicy—are part of the performance and they materially affect the way passing customers feel about what's being sold. If you're even vaguely thinking about a snack and you hear "Sweet and delicious red cherry!" you'll start picturing them in your subconscious, and you'll be imagining what they might taste like. There's a chance that your mouth may even be watering. Incredible stuff!

You need to encourage your team to use adjectives like these whenever they're talking about the products they rate highly.

▶ Awesome colors

▶ Fantastic fit

▶ Stunning design

▶ Superb taste

This does two things: It engages customers, but even better it also gives them the words they will use later to describe how pleased they are with whatever it is they've bought.

B—Merchandising

There are lessons to be learned on merchandising too—some subtle but very revealing. Fruit and vegetables on a stall tends to be laid out at an angle to the table, with orders being fulfilled from produce behind the angled crates. This arrangement makes it look like there is more food there than perhaps there really is—this is important because we animals are reassured when we see what we perceive to be "plenty." You didn't think we were influenced by that stuff, maybe? We are—all of us.

The colors of adjacent items are carefully selected too: Rather than blending harmoniously from red, to orange, to yellow, and so on, contrasting colors are put next to each other. This is to help our poor eyes pick one thing out from another and also because when you walk past this arrangement, it flickers in your peripheral vision. That flickering attracts and makes passers-by almost involuntarily glance over.

Managing perceptions is also an aspect of great retail theater—here again the fruit and vegetable sellers can do interesting things; when I wrote *Smart Retail*, I would often need to walk down Whitechapel Road and past the permanent street-market there. The market contains six greengrocers' stalls, each offering similar products. One morning I noticed lychees had arrived; these are a big draw for the greengrocers there. On five of the stalls, lychees were all presented at the front in a sort of hot spot visible to all customers.

But on the sixth stall, they weren't even on the table—this greengrocer hadn't even had time to get his lychee stock onto a shelf because it was still all on his delivery cart and customers were clamoring over it. Next day the lychees were again right out front on their delivery cart ... something didn't make sense.

I asked the stall-holder, Dinesh, why he did this. Dinesh said that customers who saw the lychees tended to believe the fruits were really fresh because they hadn't been around long enough to be taken off the delivery cart. "How fresh are they?" I asked.

"Three days, these ones."

"Do your customers really believe your lychees are fresher than everyone else's because you've not even been able to get them onto the stall?"

"Yeah, they do."

Suspending disbelief, helping customers to feel a positive thing—these are theatrical tools and you'll find ways to apply them to your business too.

Case study 14.3 Smart Retail: Theater of lardy dreams

At the height of their success, Krispy Kreme stores were taking three times more money than similarly sized Dunkin" Donut's stores. Broadly the same product (although KK reckon their recipe delivers a better texture), same sort of locations, maybe Krispy Kreme had a little bit more of an authentic brand heritage, that's marginal though.

So how come they sell so many lovely, lovely doughnuts?

Scott Livengood is the man who took the business from $200m to $1.2bn revenues in just three years. His big innovation? The introduction of a little bit of retail theater. Just like fashion—doughnuts are best when hot and fresh in-store. Livengood's moment of genius was to connect the childhood delight of hanging around the kitchen when Mom or Dad was baking with the process of buying a doughnut.

Up until Livengood's time, fresh Krispy Kreme doughnuts arrived to customers through an anonymous hatch in the wall; the machinery of cooking that doughnut was kept well out of view. Livengood recognized that watching your doughnut be cooked fresh in front of you, taking in the wonderful cooking aroma, would heighten anticipation and spike desire for the product. Stores were then redesigned to make the most of what became "doughnut theaters" and cooking times were changed from early morning to times that matched the optimum desire times—lunchtime and late afternoon—with the aromas then pumped out into the street.

A moment of truth: During a store visit, Scott witnessed a staff-member wave to a child from inside the "doughnut theater." It made the kid's day and it appeared the staff member felt good about the interaction too. Scott says that was the moment he realized that he'd done something special.

Dunkin' fight back

There is a sting in this particular tale which goes back to Big Idea. Perhaps a little slower than in the rest of the world, America is waking up to the need to eat less fat and sugar. Potentially the distant death knell for the doughnut. Krispy Kreme have failed to adapt to this change in their market and are suffering as a result.

Dunkin' Donuts, on the other hand, have moved themselves toward a coffee positioning. They have significantly improved the coffee itself, installed proper Italian coffee machines, and are now using the advertising slogan "Something fresh is always brewin' here!." It's clever: Dunkin' are now telling their customers "Hey, we're a great coffee shop but one with the most awesomely tasty snacks you'll find." It's working.

The theater of demonstration—why shopping channel presenters are unheralded geniuses

One easy way to get a bit of performance and movement into the store is to do lots of demonstrations. Again, watch market stallholders: They handle the product constantly, rotating stock, shifting clothes, rearranging sizes or colors, juggling sweets, playing music, sparking up toys, cooking spices on their hotplates. Almost every trader you see will hold a bag of product in his hand as he barks out the deal on that item—a tiny detail, but again it's done because it's useful in attracting customers.

Another great training ground for learning demonstration skills, and I am serious, is the shopping channels on TV. Watch the guest presenters especially. These are the people from the product manufacturers who get to come on and plug their wares. These men and women are brilliant instinctive performers who talk and demonstrate benefit after benefit. Now, I'm like everyone else who gets a bit annoyed when these presenters are talking up something obviously shoddy, but the techniques are still valid—imagine applying it to your best stuff, to product you genuinely believe to be great.

Helping customers to more easily imagine your product actually working for them is very powerful.

What I'm suggesting you do here is to tap into the power of everyday performance. The demonstrating and playing with stock. Customers really are drawn to products when they see life and action around them. Helping customers to more easily imagine your product actually working for them is very powerful.

Mast Brothers (Brooklyn, NY)

The brothers Mast do chocolate as performance, setting themselves and the store as a kind of crazy chocolate-twisted Norman Rockwell painting but, good God, they are authentic too. From first walking in, you see this is somewhere different: The smells are rich and powerful, your senses being triggered from the off; as well as the traditional store fittings you can see the mechanics of chocolate making going on—bars being turned out and foiled and wrapped by hand, or cocoa beans being sorted and graded by eye.

The store is only the front of a remarkable chocolate-making factory; these pioneers are one of only a handful of bean-to-bar chocolate makers in the U.S., and they will let you tour the factory at weekends (you need to pre-book and pay a tiny $9.99 for a ticket—it gets super busy). There's also a special taster room too. The store links production and product in a way that makes the end result somehow more special; Mast Brothers chocolate is exceptional without all this, but the store puts a special seal on that quality.

Apple Store (U.S.)

The entire store is built around demonstration—customers surfing the web, speakers being tried, programs shown off, videos played, music being made. The Genius Bar takes that a step further—this is where customers solve their technical problems. Now, you'd expect most retailers to want to hide their problems away but here Apple use problem-solving to add an additional layer of certainty to the purchase process—customers see that there is going to be somebody there to actually talk to if things go wrong. That's hugely valuable. And finally, a third layer of demonstration is provided through free one-hour workshops on a range of creative and productivity tasks. Show the product, show you'll solve problems, show how to get the best out of that product—that's a story, delivered theatrically, that shifts computers.

B&Q (UK)

The "You Can Do It" classes now running in a handful of B&Q stores are so popular that getting a place on forthcoming classes is a matter of luck and timing. The brilliant, brilliant aspect to these courses is that they happen on the shop floor in full view of other customers. It makes a direct link between the things B&Q sell and what those things can do for people. I'm so glad a mainstream British retailer is finally doing demonstration so well—and they're reaping the rewards: Customers who train in-store tend to fulfill more of their project needs with the store too (and, cleverly, B&Q have also introduced a free project advisor service, where a member of staff will discuss customers" needs and help them to identify everything required to get the job done). Oh, and there's a kids version of the program—the little ones get to make mug-trees, bird-feeders, and the like and they absolutely love doing it (get 'em hooked young, I getcha!).

Making it stick

Over and over we have talked about how the best of retailing is down to common sense, and to passion and gut feel. Out on the streets, on the market stalls, these components of success are in plentiful supply. They can be seen in the way stallholders price, merchandise, promote, and demonstrate. All of the lessons on display can be learned and applied to your store, whether that is a hole-in-the-wall grocer's or a 25,000 sqare foot Currys.

15

CHAPTER FIFTEEN

Detail, detail, detail—the store environment

So, we've talked about discovery and theater—now you're going to need a space to put those things in and you're going to need to think about how to lay out that space to maximum effect. There are some useful general principles in this but the detail is something you are going to have to work out for yourself, based on those principles. It's not as tricky as that might suggest, however—if you know what you are (your Big Idea), if you've worked out how you are going to deliver discovery, and if you've identified your opportunities to create some theater, then you are a good distance toward understanding how to make the physical aspect of the store work properly.

At its simplest, the store fixtures and fittings, signage, colors and windows are there to do a very simple set of things:

1 Tell customers about what you are.

2 Tempt them to come in.

3 Display products nicely.

4 Show off focus and promotional displays.

5 Lead customers through the different ranges.

6 Make it easy to select and pay for stuff.

If you can put a checkmark next to each one of those things and say "Yep, what we've got does all of those" then you're on the money already. Go at each with a lot of honest vigor though—walk through each as if you were a customer. Retail guru Martin Butler has a great expression: "Spend an hour in your customer's moccasins each day"—he's right too, you'll see things differently.

Look and feel

It's relatively easy these days to create knock-out gorgeous stores at a sensible cost. Especially as manufacturers are often keen to supply retailers with great-looking free, or part-sponsored, display systems. But even if you're spending your own money, you must match that spend to your Big Idea. A dollar store doesn't need the same level of quality or design as perhaps a boutique jeweler's. Equally, stores such as Hotel Chocolat

It's relatively easy these days to create knock-out gorgeous stores at a sensible cost.

prove that you can achieve classy results on relatively modest budgets (go have a closer look at their fixtures and fittings: They've managed to adapt some pretty standard kit and make it look amazing—that's clever retailing).

Windows

Your windows are your outside communicators and they must be made to work hard for you. So many retailers seem to think this either means filling them with meaningless piles of stock or filling them with a billion confusing messages.

A good window display is critical. It must be welcoming: It must give passers-by new reasons to come in, and it has to be readable in five seconds. New products are great as window features. When I asked the owner of a successful hardware store how he promoted his hot new items, he said "I put them in the window with a great sign on them that says 'bargain' and 'brand-new' on it. Customers notice the sign. I know they do because they ask me about these new products and then they buy them." And, of course, seasonal or special-occasion activity must be celebrated in your windows too.

Broadly, your windows can do three things, either individually or in combination. They can do the following.

Intrigue

Abstract but sharply focused images that pique customers" interest. A great example of this can be seen in many AllSaints stores where the main window features rows and rows of old sewing machines. It is a theatrical intrigue, makes people want to know what's going on, and has the psychological bonus that in customers" subconscious, it suggests tailoring, hand-making, and quality—all of which helps support AllSaints" premium positioning.

Inform

Simple and sharp messages often accompanied by a single product: Sale Now On, Our Best Ever Jacket $99, New Stock Preview. Orange does these very well and change theirs every week. You can do the same using cheap but professional vinyl lettering.

Inspire

A window that gets customers thinking about the store and its contents. Gap had a terrific one recently: three fun spring dresses in the window with a great typographical treatment that just said "Flirty Dresses Are The Key To Spring." That's inspiring—it instantly has the customer thinking about ditching the winter blues and jumping into a fun spring wardrobe.

Case study 15.1 Smart Retail: PetSmart performance

Walk up to PetSmart's Broadway store and you'll usually see a little crowd of people peering into the window. You might even stop to stare too—for one part of that window looks directly in on their pet-grooming room. You'll see pampered pooches having their coats trimmed, their claws nipped, and all manner of other crazy pet nonsense. New Yorkers love it, and it's a brilliant example of a window that both intrigues and inspires—it makes you look and it tells you that PetSmart love your pets.

My all-time favorite window is also one of the simplest I've ever seen: It's this understated and fun masterpiece from Paul Smith—you can't see the shoes. Almost everyone walks over to take a look.
Source: Koworld

Transition zone

This is the area near the door that transfers customers from the outside and then into the store. You have an opportunity here to make or break the customer experience. If the zone is too empty, customers can feel exposed and then reluctant to move further into the store. If it's too cluttered, that's off-putting too—instead it should be clear and easy but with things of interest in it to draw people in gently.

You also need to be aware throughout the store, but here especially, of what retail anthropologist Paco Underhill calls the "butt-brush factor." He noticed that customers hate standing anywhere that puts them at risk of other customers constantly brushing past them. In the transition zone, this effect can be useful because it keeps people moving forward on into the store. In front of displays, though, it can be a problem because you want customers to linger in those areas. When they do linger, they tend to buy more often. Take a look at all the customer flows in your store, from the entrance and back out again, to see where you can make improvements.

Baskets

If yours is a store where customers ever need to pick up more than one item, then you must offer baskets. Customers who pick up a basket nearly always buy something and very often buy more than customers who don't have a basket. Stores always benefit from having baskets available invitingly on the side edges of the transition zone.

Put the baskets higher up, not on the floor. Perching baskets on a table makes it very easy for your customers to just dangle an arm down and almost absent-mindedly pick up a basket. Doing so will increase sales and average transaction values.

Promotional hot spots

Creative use of promotions is essential. Fill the store with them, show people excellent value, and then make it easy for them to take you up on your brilliant offers. Never allow a promotion spot to go empty: If you have run out of a line, even for just a few hours, get the promotion POS off the floor right now. If you don't, you will annoy customers who will feel you have let them down.

The ideal promotional hot spots are:

▶ Visible from the door

▶ Well lit

▶ Bristling with stock

▶ Easy to linger in front of

▶ Honestly presented

▶ Clearly merchandised

▶ Well signed

▶ Surprising

Promotional product can mean a lot of different things, remember, such as:

▶ Price offers

▶ Products we want to showcase because we love them

▶ New acquisitions

▶ Seasonal favorites

▶ Things that go together (preferable with a package price)

▶ New ideas

▶ Products in the news

▶ Hot trend items.

A good tip in a small store is to reserve a space that's in customers" immediate eye-line when they come in through the front door, and use that to showcase a changing selection. Mark it as such, make it clear, and both regulars and new customers alike will make it their first stop on each visit.

Back wall

Do you remember how record shops always used to feature the top twenty singles up on the back wall? That was so they could draw every customer the right way through the store. The really savvy stores would make it very easy for customers to walk through the middle of the shop to the back wall, so customers would all be flowing down that central aisle. Then when a customer had found their chosen single, they would turn and look for the cash register. This would be placed back up toward the doors. The customer couldn't easily walk back along the central aisle because it was full of people heading toward them, so they would zigzag through the displays to either side. This zigzagging was brilliant because it meant the customer was exposed to a whole succession of promotional hot spots as they navigated their indirect course.

Cash register

There are lots of arguments over where best to put cash registers. To be honest all have their pros and cons. My preferred position is halfway down one side wall. You can see most of the store from there, queuing can be dealt with neatly and it doesn't eat into the best selling areas.

Here are the most popular options:

▶ Halfway down one side—my favorite.

▶ At the front to one side—makes it easy to greet customers walking in but puts the desk right in the middle of important promotional space.

▶ In a center island—although islands can break up sight-lines, this can work really well, especially if you are able to have two people working the desk most of the time because the pair can then watch half the store each, giving you full visual cover.

▶ On the back wall—popular really only because it usually puts staff near back-of-house areas; makes it hard to greet customers and is the shoplifters" favorite option because staff are so far from the door.

Impulse buys

Whatever you sell there will be products in your range that will make great register impulse purchases. In a newsstand, chocolate is an obvious example. Hip clothing stores will put cheap toys and iconic trinkets on the counter. Anything that is attractive, low-cost, and that is physically small will make a great impulse purchase. Vary your selections a little and don't crowd the area. A few well-chosen items can have a direct impact on increasing your average transaction values. Avoid at all costs the hideously

> **Anything that is attractive, low-cost, and that is physically small will make a great impulse purchase.**

uncomfortable joke of forcing your staff to actively sell these items—staff at WHSmith are made to ask customers if they would like "Any half-price chocolate today, sir?" They hate having to do it and customers are made to feel uncomfortable. It's pushy and weird.

Sight-lines

Two considerations here are foremost:

1   Can customers see their way around the store?
2   Can you see them?

Customers like to be drawn through your space by the exciting and attractive products and promotions you put in their middle-distance forward vision even as their brains fight to pay greater attention to the peripheral and to movement. They will often miss things that are right next to them unless you lead them right to the spot.

Being able to see customers is important because it makes it easy for you and the team to acknowledge them. It is also vital in reducing shoplifting. If you can see the thief better, they are less able to steal—simple as that.

Signage

Always go for crisp and readable over complex, over-designed, or wordy. Customers just do not have the time or inclination to decipher clever complicated messages. Promotional signage especially should convey a strong bold message in just a few seconds. Ratty signage does nothing for your store—if POS gets damaged, throw it away or replace it immediately.

So, the fundamental principles are covered, but the rest is up to you— exciting times!

16

And finally ...
how we got here

I want to finish the store section of the book with a look at the history of retail. It doesn't properly fit here but I didn't want to relegate it to an appendix either. This stuff is important and it will help you to be a better retailer. The lessons are all there for us.

Righty ho—I'm going to take us through the early years, up to somewhere around the 1950s. There are a few reasons for doing that—the first is to prove a really important point: Retailing is not about inventing new stuff.

Eh? "But you've gone on and on about ideas being the lifeblood of retailing and that ..."

That's true, I have—here's the thing: Ideas are of course vital, ideas are about change, improvement, and development, but they are rarely about coming up with things that no human has ever thought about before. You can be an innovative retailer by improving on existing ideas, by combining existing practices in radical new ways. But you don't have to magically pluck brand-new "things" out of nowhere to be innovative and successful.

And this is a good thing. I'm going to show you over the course of this section that there have only really been four important inventions in retailing over the last 2200 years. This should be liberating for you—what I'm, in effect, saying is that you don't have to reinvent the wheel to be innovative.

Rather than make you guess—I'll give them to you for free. The four great inventions in retail are:

- ▶ c.200 BC—the creation of the first chain of stores (China)
- ▶ 17th century—catalog-based mail-order (Europe)

- 1852—the first true "department" store (France)
- 1915/16—self-service (U.S.)

That's it. Yeah, maybe we're overdue something else earth-shattering and new sometime soon; maybe it'll be you that invents it, but if it's not—that's okay! It's not vital to your success as a retailer. Oh, and if anyone is shouting "Idiot! Hammond's missed out the Internet," calm yourselves down: The Internet is just a development of catalog-based mail order and don't kid yourself that it isn't—it's all distance selling.

On that point, right here in St. Albans where I'm happily typing away, there's an excellent 19th-century analog to the current thinking among leading Internet players around becoming bricks-and-mortar retailers: On our original main street, there's a beautiful white glass, brick, and iron-frame building. It looks like a cross between a massive greenhouse and a Victorian bath. Actually, it was built more than a hundred years ago as a showroom for the leading mail-order seed catalog of the time—it was a place where the seeds could be shown off as plants, where arrangements of flowers, trees, and shrubs could be suggested to customers and in which expert growers could pass on their tips. Isn't that

Our retail past informs our retail present.

wonderful? You see—our retail past informs our retail present. The seed showroom is a Café Rouge now. Not sure what that says about the future of amazon.com!

I reckon there are two good reasons for giving you a bit of retail history: The first is to give you the reassurance that you're not trying to invent something nobody has thought of before; the second is to show you that the challenges you face have all been solved before and that you can learn from those earlier experiences.

Actually, there's a third and perhaps more personal reason for pulling together this brief history—and it's that I believe retail is important and that the heroes of retail should be celebrated and their accomplishments enjoyed as we carve out our own retail successes.

The really early days

So, to the history. Our retail trade predates money—money comes later, having grown out of the need to mark retail debt in a consistent manner. What you do really is one of the oldest professions.

Markets

The first formal gatherings of retail outlets were barter-based markets. Within a community, specialist skills developed—one producer who had a skill, say, in stone implements would deliberately over-produce these so that he could swap his spares for food or clothing with specialists in those areas.

Retail chains

That brings us to the concept of the chain-store. It's an interesting evolution—as the markets became more permanent and currency arrived, it made sense to construct a logistical infrastructure around those fixed points, the markets. Successful fixed-location shopkeepers recognized that growing their square footage (or square cubits, or whatever) and growing their potential customer-base represented excellent opportunities to make a little more profit. The answer was to open up another shop and have it operated by a family member. And would you believe, even back then there are records of these fledgling chain-store businesses using their improved volumes to leverage better terms from suppliers.

The earliest reasonable claim to "first retail chain" can be found in China over 2200 years ago and belongs to a retailer called Lo Kass. There is also a strong possibility that Roman shopkeepers may have a prior claim but only Lo Kass's is actually documented. Roman excavations, across the empire, have shown that shops there were extraordinarily like small shops are today and given the excellent formal government, commercial, and transport infrastructures present even early-on in the Roman period, it's pretty likely that chains emerged there. Lo Kass's innovation, the thing that allowed him to extend his business, is that he was the first recorded retailer to employ shop managers from outside of his family.

Family to formal

Two things held back the small chains from making the leap to vast multiple retailers—the lack of non-familial trustworthy workers and audit systems to keep them so, and the lack of long-distance mechanised travel. It wasn't until the Industrial Revolution had really hit, in the 19th century, that chains became much bigger and more widespread. A few of those pioneer chains still exist today.

Places of retail

Generally, retailing has always taken place at the heart of communities. Markets were central points in villages and inside the largest cities markets would spring up, centered on shared-interest locations—animal markets in one quarter, grain in another, cloth elsewhere, and so on.

Main streets, U.S.-style suburban strip-malls, and indoor town-center shopping malls (or centers) are the direct descendants of those community markets. The one major, late 20th century change to retail location history is the out-of-town shopping mall and the edge-of-town retail parks—we'll talk about those a little more in a moment.

But the structure of malls themselves have been with us since the Romans. Dr. John Dawson (Professor of Retailing at Stirling University and a great retail brain) points out that the ruins of Trajan's Market in Rome are remarkably similar to a modern urban mall. He goes on to mention that this particular market continued to operate in the same way throughout the Middle Ages and into modernity.

Later, much later, we get recognizably modern, though still very similar to Trajan's Market, mall-style arcades including the Burlington Arcade in London, opened in 1819. The Arcade in Providence, Rhode Island introduced the concept to the United States in 1828. The larger Galleria Vittorio Emanuele II in Milan, Italy followed in the 1860s.

The move away from high streets

Suburban living, commuting, and the rise of the road and car has given rise to a move away from shopping on high streets. Throughout the 1990s and especially in the U.S., the center of retail has moved from the old high streets and into giant regional shopping malls and to massive stores located in retail parks on the edge of towns.

Lack of space has, to an extent, halted this move in Western Europe but even in spacious North America, something interesting is happening—main streets are thriving once more. Indeed main-street rents in the U.S. are increasing at an astonishing rate—rents tend to mirror commercial success and so are a useful barometer of location health.

It would appear that there is something fundamental about humans and shopping and doing so inside our communities (however superficial those communities may be). Fashion, food, entertainment, small-specialist, personal technology, personal services, and gift retailers will thrive again at the center of our communities and on our main streets—the added value of convenience, immediacy, and shopping in mixed, varied, and stimulating locations is rising.

Department stores

The development of department stores is important because it marks the first real, systematic, use of retail theater—and it's that theater that has driven almost every single customer-facing innovation since. It is the absolute key component of modern format-planning and concept development. It is what sorts the mediocre from the fantastic.

Until 1852, shops were all small and specialist. That changed forever when Aristide Boucicaut and his wife Marguerite expanded their Parisian drapery store and began to also sell housewares and bed linen. They called their store Le Bon Marché and its inception marked the birth of the world's first department store. The store launched on the back of innovations such as the promise to deliver "to homes as far as a horse can travel in Paris" and for the first time anywhere the store featured prices clearly written on all labels. The Boucicauts are even credited with the invention of modern stock management, where rotating merchandise and the staging of summer sales, winter sales, and blue-cross sales created constant change and excitement in the store.

Then in 1869, Bon Marché moved into stunning new purpose-built premises, designed in part by Gustave Eiffel, in the rue de Sèvres. Imagine how you might have felt the charge strike through you the first time you walked through the huge iron and glass doors and into its fabulous interior. Just imagine that thrill; stunning clothes, awe-inspiring furniture, drapery from all corners of the earth, sweets like you have

**The Grands Magasins du Bon Marché was the world's first
department store. This photograph was taken in 1928.**
Source: Royal Institute of British Architects Picture Archives

never seen before, foodstuffs to make the mind boggle, and baffling new gadgets you cannot begin to fathom the workings of. You see assistants bustling here and there, catwalk displays of clothes, and dressed mannequins among showmen demonstrating the latest wonder. Every turn holds something new, a surprise, a wondrous assault on the senses. Imagine too how amazing it felt as you discovered that every department, as well as showing you awesome delights you'd never known existed, had lots of nice things in them that you could afford. Bon Marché changed its ranges constantly; new surprises were guaranteed all the time. It's a product mix and stock management philosophy that worked then and still holds true today.

The concept of browsing a store was alien to the masses before 1852. It just was not a part of the contemporary ritual of shopping. Today browsers are essential to everyone from Wal-Mart to Harrods. That's why we pack our stores with hot spots and why we change things so often. It's all down to Bon Marché and their astonishing 19th-century Parisian innovations.

The concept of browsing a store was alien to the masses before 1852.

Well, that's not entirely true. One other major, seismic, earthquake of change needed to happen and that was the development of self-service shopping. The established retail model, even within multi-department stores such as Bon Marché, was to keep products in cases, behind counters, or under glass—customers would be served by an assistant who would fetch customers" products for them.

Self-service

This all changed in 1915 when Albert Gerrard opened the Groceteria in Los Angeles, the first documented self-service store. The early part of the twentieth century was an extraordinarily competitive time in general-store retail in the U.S., but even in that white-heat environment, it took almost a year for another operator to copy the idea. And what a copy it was! Clarence Saunders, the founder of Tennessee-based Piggly Wiggly, built an entire business around self-service and then, the sly fellow, went and secured a patent on the concept (I've not been able to discover if that patent was ever enforced—I quite enjoy the thought of one of his long-lost relatives appearing out of the woodwork and suing all the grocers).

Saunders was something of a legendary loon and had begun construction of a pink marble mansion in Memphis, Tennessee when in 1932 the "bears" of Wall Street allegedly took him for a million dollars and rendered him personally bankrupt. The "Pink Palace" is now a museum, and it includes a walk-through model of the first Piggly Wiggly store, complete with 2¢ packets of Kellogg's cornflakes and 8¢ cans of Campbell's soup. It's well worth a visit—the place shows you what a real retail innovation actually looks like.

And that's where I'm going to leave the history for now and move on instead to the stories of some of the most important pioneers of our trade.

The retail kings

Say hello to the retail kings—these men are the true pioneers of your trade. They had no maps, instead forging their own routes through opportunity and adversity alike. There are a couple of sad endings, mind you—so be prepared for that.

Self-service as shown in Saunders" patent grant no. 1,242,872.
Source: US Patent Office

George Hartford and George Gilman—A&P (U.S.)

The Great Atlantic & Pacific Tea Company, better known as A&P, is the original American supermarket chain. The company was founded by George Hartford and George Gilman. By 1876, A&P had 67 stores, increasing to 1,000 by 1915. In the 1920s and 1930s, the company utterly dominated the American retail market, and by the end of that period, A&P was operating approximately 16,000 stores with combined revenue of $1 billion. That power led to the U.S. Congress passing several anti-predatory pricing laws—it's interesting to see pressure on governments today to act in a similar manner in order to curb the practices of some of our most powerful supermarket chains.

That 1930s high has now, to a large extent, evaporated—A&P still trades today but from far fewer locations and it is far from the biggest retailer in the U.S. now.

In 1859, Gilman opened The Great American Tea Company, a corner shop, on Vesey Street in Lower Manhattan (the site today of Ground Zero). The

A typical small A&P—this one is at L'Anse, Michigan—1950s.
Source: A&P Historical Society

store sold teas, coffees, spices, baking powder, condensed milk—all products that often came to America as ballast in the holds of clipper ships. The name change came in the 1870s when the company began to ship goods via the transcontinental railroad—with their broadened horizons, connecting "Atlantic" and "Pacific" must have seemed like an extraordinary achievement.

What marks out Hartford and Gilman from other retailers of the time is their voracious expansion ambition and achievement, and the way they overlaid that on a consistent format. They knew what customers wanted and delivered a store that met those needs—again and again, in location after location. Even today, the vast bulk of American retailers remain regionalized but the two Georges blitzed out those 16,000 nationwide, coast-to-coast, stores by 1937.

F.W. Woolworth—Woolworths (U.S.)

Franklin Winfield Woolworth (born on April 13, 1852, died on April 8, 1919) was *the* American merchant. Born in Rodman, New York, he was the founder of F.W. Woolworth Company, an operator of discount stores that eventually settled into the Big Idea of pricing merchandise at five and ten cents (making it a "five-and-dime" store). He pioneered the now-common practice of buying merchandise direct from manufacturers and was among the first retailers to fix prices on all items rather than haggle as was the prevailing tradition. Woolworth was also among the first retailers to recognize the potential in selling mass-produced products. Clever man, this Mr. Woolworth! F.W. was one of the first retailers to truly understand his customers—he recognized that this business is about consistency, choice, and democracy (good stuff, at the right price, for all).

Woolworth grew up on a farm but something sparked the retail bug in him pretty early on, and it was while working at a dry-goods store that he had his first great idea. He noticed that leftover items were often priced at five cents and placed on a table to get rid of them; he noted how much customers seemed to appreciate the five-cent table and a light went on in his brain … Woolworth then borrowed $300 to open his own store in which all items were priced at five cents.

That first store, in Utica, New York, opened on February 22, 1879, and failed before the end of March. At his second store, in Lancaster, Pennsylvania (opened in April 1879), he adjusted the format by expanding the concept to include another range of merchandise priced at ten cents. This second range balanced the offer better and the Lancaster store became a big success. Woolworth and his brother, Charles Sumner Woolworth, solidified the template and then went on to open a large number of their five-and-dime stores.

The concept was widely copied, and five-and-dime stores were a fixture in the average American downtown for the first half of the 20th century, and they then later anchored suburban strip malls.

Always loving the grand gesture, in 1913 Woolworth built the Woolworth Building in New York City at a cost of $13.5 million (which he paid in cash). At the time, it was the tallest building in the world, at a height of 792 feet, or 241.4 meters. The Chrysler Building, with its craftily constructed spire, robbed Woolworth of that record the same year. Can you imagine the sheer balls of a man prepared to make a statement on the scale of the Woolworth Building? I love that—it's madness, but it's wonderful too.

The Woolworth Building in New York.
Source: AP/Press Association

As well as its American success, Woolworths extended across into lots of other countries—in the UK, "Woolies" became a fixture of everyday life. It provided ordinary families, like mine, with nice things at a very low price. The quality was reliable and the range mind-blowing: some 70,000 different lines by the start of the 1980s.

Woolworth died in April 1919 at the age of 66. At the time, his company owned more than 1,000 stores and was a $65 million corporation. Ten years earlier, he had opened his first British Woolworths, in Liverpool. He went on to personally open 50 UK stores before his death. Opening these stores himself, especially accounting for the time it took to travel between the U.S. and the UK back then, showed F.W.'s extraordinary commitment to consistency.

Stunningly, all that's left of the original company, following a mass store-closure in 1997, is the Foot Locker chain (originally a Woolworths' sub-brand). The South African, German, NZ, and large Australian Woolworths' are very, very distant cousins, having all been independent of F.W. Woolworth and of each other for decades.

Ingvar Kamprad—IKEA (Sweden)

Ingvar Kamprad was born in Sweden on March 30, 1926 and is the founder of IKEA, having opened the first store in 1943. Not entirely sure why, but the earliness of that date surprises me every time I see it. Modern as it feels, IKEA has a long history, and it is thoroughly imbued with the benefits of evolution over a nice long timeline.

Ingvar developed his first business as a boy, selling matches to neighbors from his bicycle. He found that he could buy matches in bulk very cheaply from Stockholm, sell them individually at a low price, and still make a good profit. From matches, he expanded to selling fish, Christmas tree decorations, seeds, and later ballpoint pens and pencils. When Ingvar was 17, his father gave him a little cash for doing well at school. He used this cash to establish what has grown into IKEA.

Early IKEA was very much about opportunist retail, selling whatever it could, but the big growth came after Kamprad started to think systematically about selling furniture. His guiding philosophy came to be "A better life everyday for the majority of people." I think he meant it too: IKEA is much more than the generation of profits. It offers good things to lots of people at a low cost and without class distinctions. It is accessible, exciting, and honest.

The story of why IKEA customers go into a warehouse area to pick up their furniture is a great illustration of why this company is a great one. In the early days of IKEA, you didn't do that: A helper went and found your stuff for you. Then in 1965, they opened a big new store in Stockholm and on the first day, sales went crazy. There were more customers than the store could handle. Things were awful at the collection area. So the store manager made a judgement call: He opened up the warehouse and allowed customers to come in and find their own items. It worked so well that they tried it again another day, and the rest is history. In IKEA, that manager was recognized for having improved the way the store worked. Anywhere else and he'd have been reprimanded for breaking the rules.

In 1978, Kamprad wrote his seminal retail manifesto "Testament of a Furniture Dealer." In it you read statements such as "to make mistakes is the privilege of the active person. Only while asleep does one make no

A typical IKEA store.
Source: AP/Press Association/Herbert Proepper

mistakes" and "an idea without a price tag is unacceptable." That character is strong in IKEA all over the world. It is so strong that it can be made to cross cultural borders. IKEA in Croydon is as recognisable in its IKEA-ness as IKEA in Gothenburg. I truly believe IKEA to be the best retail company to have ever opened its doors to a customer—it has become almost the sole source for furnishings for many households across the world, though there is some evidence now that competitors are emerging who can challenge IKEA.

There's a word of caution here, and that's the risk of ubiquity. There is a backlash beginning to rise against "IKEA style" in which a home furnished exclusively by IKEA is considered to be a bit cheap. My single criticism of IKEA is that the company hasn't moved its design forward fast enough. We've had nearly a decade of the IKEA revolution in the UK and the products seem to be broadly similar now to the early days.

My single criticism of IKEA is that the company hasn't moved its design forward fast enough.

Sam Walton—Wal-Mart (U.S.)

Sam Walton, the founder of Wal-Mart, was a customer genius. More than that, in creating the world's biggest company (not just the biggest retailer), he also showed how to create a consistency of culture that is truly gob-smacking. Every single member of the worldwide Wal-Mart team knows exactly what the company does, how it should do that, and why. The stores are packed with bargains, dependable value, and lots of things to make customers smile.

Wal-Mart is, however, facing pressures from home-grown challengers such as Target as well as encountering strong competitors in critical overseas markets (Aldi, for one, drove Wal-Mart out of Germany in 2006). Some of the Sam magic appears to be slipping away from the company (Walton died in 1992). U.S. employee unrest in particular is fast becoming a serious issue—it needs addressing before it's too late, and before the goodwill that broadly does still exist within the workforce is further eroded.

Those are the clouds on the horizon—largely issues after Sam's time—dealt with. Let's get back to the good stuff: Sam Walton's great legacy is everyday low pricing. As an early operator of franchised Ben Franklin five-and-dime stores, Walton made the unilateral decision to cut margins to the bone in a drive for volume. He chose everyday products on which to focus his most aggressive price discounting: toothpaste and ladies" pants were among his favorite and most successful choices. The simple observation that it was better to sell a ton of product at low margin than to sell a small volume at a high margin drove the almost unchallenged sixty years of Wal-Mart growth.

Some of Walton's most innovative ideas aren't around promotion or price but relate to his work on cutting costs (savings that he then always passed on to customers). He was the first to offer his store managers a profit-share—essentially he said, "It's your business; manage it as such and you will receive a share in the success." Walton recognized that this would make his managers focus more on controllable costs, on taking advantage of product opportunities, and on reducing shrinkage. Another Walton innovation is the "greeter"—a member of staff standing in the entranceway to stores welcoming customers in. This system (which was

Sam Walton's original store: now the Wal-Mart Visitor Center, Bentonville, Arkansas.
Source: Bobak Ha'Eri

actually introduced first by one of Walton's managers as a temporary thing but recognized by Walton as a valuable permanent practice) dramatically cut customer theft at the same time as making arriving customers feel a little bit more important.

Though price became an absolute obsession for Walton, I don't believe it was ever a greed thing. I'm convinced that driving the focus on price was Sam's heartfelt belief that ordinary people should always get the best possible deal. It was an honest proposition that made him and his family an awful lot of money but that also reduced the cost of everyday items for hard-working honest citizens.

Wal-Mart has always attracted criticism from smaller retailers who accuse the company of exploiting their buying power to drive high-street and local retailers out of business. To an extent that's true, and it's why I believe that some measure of government control on monopoly and single-center retail power is sensible, but that's only half the story. Many, not all but many, of those retailers who go bust in the wake of a Wal-Mart opening are doing so because they fail to offer their customers anything particularly special—there's no added value there. Walton himself challenged small retailers to quit the bellyaching and "Work out what you can do that we can't and then get really good at that thing and get really good at telling your customers about it."

Quite right. That's good advice—get busy living!

The Gordon Selfridge method—Selfridges & Co. (UK)

American Harry Gordon Selfridge opened a large store in London's Oxford Street on March 15, 1909 and named it Selfridges (the current store, frontage included, is larger still, having been extended some time later). A clean-living dedicated man, Selfridge came alive when on the shop floor— he went from accountant to showman and is the true father of great retail theater. Indeed the resurgence of the once-moribund 1970s Selfridges is entirely down to another great retail entertainer—Vittorio Raddice. The key to Selfridges" early success was Gordon's decision to move products out from behind the counters and to make them accessible to customers. He wanted shoppers to be able to touch, explore, and be excited by products (before an assistant then helped the customer to actually make the final selection—true self-service still being six years, and a continent, away).

The man and his store, Vanity Fair—1911.
Source: National Portrait Gallery, London

A key component in the Selfridges format was staff behavior: He wanted them to be accessible but never aggressive, knowledgeable but never smug. He is the man most often credited with originating the phrase "The customer is always right"—an edict that permeated throughout the customer experience in-store. To be fair, I'm not sure we really know who first actually said that, but Gordo will do for now. Selfridge also recognized that he could make as much money delighting the less well off as from selling crazy curios to the rich. In this way, Selfridges was a democratizer—it was a store that welcomed and treated all customers equally. That simply had not happened before and is an important lesson in how to spread your appeal without diluting your brand.

Selfridge recognized the power of wonder to drive customer traffic and was always on the hunt for grand opportunities to demonstrate the world's cutting edge. In 1909, after the first cross-Channel flight, Louis Blériot's monoplane was exhibited in the store, where it was seen by 12,000 people. The first public demonstration of television was by John Logie Baird from the first floor of Selfridges in 1925. Just two examples in a long history—Raddice brought this sense of occasion back to the store with a series of powerful events and themes. Of late, these themed events haven't quite felt as creative, passionate, or authentic as they did under Raddice. Selfridges in the period up to 2005 was the best store in the world, but it isn't right now. I hope that changes.

Back to Gordon: He was born in Wisconsin on January 11, 1858. In 1879, he joined the retail firm of Field, Leiter and Company (which later became the legendary Marshall Field and Company). Over the next twenty-five years, Selfridge worked his way up the commercial ladder. He was appointed a junior partner and made a significant pot of capital for himself as well as successfully helping to manage the business.

His move to the UK was a huge gamble, really dramatic stuff, and came after he'd taken a holiday in London in 1906. He and Mrs. Selfridge had been utterly underwhelmed by the retail offerings in London and over the next few years, Selfridge plotted a return: this time as a retailer rather than a customer. In 1909, he came back to London with $400,000 capital and chose to invest it by building his own department store in what was then the unfashionable western end of Oxford Street.

I'm as much fascinated by the man as by his store—he was a great retail entertainer, understood inside and out the importance of surprise, discovery, delight, and "wow" but in his formal business dealings and in his private life, he was hugely restrained and at all times absolutely professional.

And then, in 1918, Mrs. Selfridge died.

Gordon went wild in the most splendid fashion. First off, he began to spend extravagantly, abandoned his teetotal tradition, and maintained a busy social life with lavish parties at his home in Lansdowne House in Berkeley Square. He bought Highcliffe Castle in Hampshire and promptly moved in a set of music-hall lovelies, triplet sisters as the story goes, and appears to have kept them as handy mistresses. It was almost as if Selfridge had finally given in to his own heady retail dream and decided to let it rule him.

But what goes up and all that: During the years of the Great Depression, Gordon watched his fortune evaporate—not helped by his gambling habit. In 1941, he was forced out of the Selfridges business, moved from his mansion, and in 1947 he died in absolute poverty at Putney in south-west London. The old man was regularly sighted, in tramp's clothing, outside the Selfridges store toward the end—a sad end to a stunning life.

Epilogue—And we're done?

Again! Thanks for that—I hope you enjoyed reading *Smart Retail* as much as I did writing it. This is a practical book and I would like to think that you are out there putting this stuff into practice as we speak. Please let me have your feedback: on the stuff you didn't like as well as on the bits you've got something out of. Tips on other great retailers for me to go and take a look at are always welcome too—especially ones outside the UK and U.S.

Further Smart Retail
Smart Retail speaking

Nothing brings this stuff to life like me turning up and passionately talking about it—I've got a set of insight-filled, idea-packed, and practical talks that send delegates away buzzing and motivated.

The Smart Retail Seminars

Practical, proven, and effective—my team and I deliver a set of superb training seminars. Our induction day is legendary and our Street Time Live day in which we take your people structured-shopping is one of the most powerful things I've ever been involved in. Always tailored to your business, market, and objectives, these seminars are spot on.

Consultancy

Our bread and butter comes from solving specific problems—if something's keeping you up at night, or you've spotted an opportunity, or you want to bring in a wider perspective, then get in touch and we will build you a great solution.

The Wednesday Clinic

Most Wednesday mornings, I give away my time free to any retailer who wants a little bit of it. I'm happy to talk about anything you want: store problems, ideas, opportunities, confusions—anything. I see it as my chance to give back a tiny bit to the industry that's given me so much. If you want a bit of this time one Wednesday morning, send me an email and I'll give you the phone number to call.

My email: richard@smart-circle.com
Web: www.Smart-Circle.com
Twitter: TheseRetailDays
Foursquare: TheseRetailDays
Facebook: Smart Retail

Thank you for buying and reading *Smart Retail*.

All the best,
Richard

Richard Hammond—Spires Shopping Center, Barnet.
Source: Stillwater Rock

Your job and *Smart Retail*

The book is written from the point of view of an enterprising store manager in a chain. That's for the sake of clarity and expediency, but I know that retailers of all levels use the book, which is great. Here are a few thoughts on how to get the best from *Smart Retail* whatever your role in the business.

Store manager

Most of you who manage stores will be working for a chain. If that's a small chain, you will have lots of opportunity to influence important aspects of the store. You may be able to persuade an owner to introduce new lines or to run certain promotions. If that's the case, you can read this book as an owner.

You may instead be one manager out of a hundred, or out of six hundred for that matter. It can feel really hard sometimes to get your voice heard. Don't let that hold you back—eventually people do notice—keep pushing yourself forward, build a strong team, and make sure key people understand why your store works as well as it does.

In particular, trust me on this: If you follow the "Team" section of the book closely, you will improve your store's performance significantly. It's the most powerful stuff in retail.

Store owner

You're in a fantastic position; you're able to vary any aspect of your business that you want to. You have free rein in this book. Sometimes you will need to spend money on your business, but I am a strong believer in the notion that many things you might need to do can be done at low cost—so it's not all bad.

As is the case for the chain-store manager, all of the advice and ideas on people management can be applied directly for free, and are presented in a practical and obvious way. This means that either you or your managers can make a significant positive impact on the business right away without spending a penny, which is nice.

Team member

There are lots of different reasons why we go into retail: Let's be honest, those reasons might include necessity and convenience. I reckon there's a chance, though, that you might just be in it for something more: After all, you've bought a book on retail; you're getting hooked by it. That makes you very important to me. This book is the tool that will help you to accelerate your retail career. Use it to make suggestions in team meetings; use it to develop your leadership skills and your retail instincts.

Many of the sections and chapters in *Smart Retail* deal with the fundamentals of retail: A good knowledge of these will make you very attractive to employers as you progress your career. To help you get the complete picture, it really is worth going through the whole book in order, front to back at least once. Sorry to sound a bit like your Dad.

As you read, try to consider things from a store manager's point of view; by doing that, you will find it much easier to pitch your ideas to your actual manager. I've also built some of the action plans in a way that means you can easily adapt them to make great interview presentations. This is especially useful when you are chasing a promotion or applying for a job with a new team.

Assistant store manager (ASM)

You are the backbone of retail management: Without good ASMs many stores just do not work. I hope you are alongside a good manager. If you are, that person will value your input and it will be easy for you to make *Smart Retail* work your way. Luckily most of you will be working in good teams and for good people, so use this opportunity to make some positive noise. Make good use of the planning tools provided here and you will gain lots from *Smart Retail*.

Area/regional manager

As one of the few people in the company who spends time both in stores and with the senior management team, you are in a unique position. You have the opportunity to make a big impact on the overall success of the business.

It is a pressure role, and *Smart Retail* can help you to deliver ideas and strategies that keep your boss happy and that can help you to feel that you are actually moving the business forward. You are one of the audiences that I put most thought into when constructing the book—have a long think hard about introducing the ideas in the "Team" section especially. You've also got a good opportunity to use *Smart Retail* to benchmark the way your business operates.

Central functions (marketing, sales operations, administration, and so on)

If you started your retail career in a shop, at the worksite, then you'll enjoy reading *Smart Retail*. Many of the stories and ideas will bring back some, hopefully, good memories. Other sections could well act as useful updates to your experience.

If you have never worked in a shop, then this is the best look into in-store reality you could ever hope for. No matter how good your marketing consultancy, there is no substitute for a proper understanding of what life in-store is really like. *Smart Retail* will give you that.

If you're the type who feels a study visit to the local street-market is beneath you, then this book is not for you. On the other hand, if you are desperate to find effective ways to gain new competitive advantage, to improve customer experiences, or to build better teams, then this may just prove to be the best money you'll ever invest.

Notes for all readers

Above all, *Smart Retail* is a practical proposition. You don't have to read the whole thing or slavishly follow directions like they were the ingredients and instructions for making a cake or something. Just pick out that one thing today that you can make a difference to, then another tomorrow, and another the day after. Before very long, you will find that these baby steps have begun to add up to a significant journey of change and improvement.

APPENDIX II
Take-action time

Smart Retail is all about the practical. I urge you, please, have a crack at this little personal exercise which is designed to get you started on the route to change. I like selling lots of books, but that process is only really rewarding when I hear that readers have actually used them to make positive moves forward. This exercise is an effective way to kick-start that.

Quickly write down the answers to these four questions. Do it automatically, without over-thinking it. Try to keep writing continuously without pausing. Once you've done that, then you can go back over them and do some trimming and tidying. Tackling this exercise this way helps you to be more honest and more practical in your choices.

▶ What five things have jumped out at you from the pages of this book?

▶ What is the first thing you plan to do tomorrow morning?

▶ What objectives will you set for yourself over the rest of the month?

▶ What are the changes you want to see in your own management style this year? How will you make these changes?

Time plan

And now, more formally, spend a little time filling out this timed plan. Please be honest, stretching, and practical.

One month after I finish reading *Smart Retail*, I will have achieved these goals:

1.

2.

3.

4.

5.

When we get to six months, these changes will have taken place:

1.

2.

3.

After a year, these important long-term changes will be evident:

1.

2.

APPENDIX III
Street time

This is a day we run as part of our training programs—normally we obviously try to dress it up a bit with all sorts of important words such as "structured," "energizing," and "experiential." Clients like that sort of guff for some reason. Between you and me: This exercise is about going shopping. It's good fun when done with a group, and it always uncovers loads of ideas and gets people thinking creatively. It can be quite shocking—I've had a number of top retailers give the feedback that they hadn't really seen shops as customers see them in years.

What do we do?

Ideally run it with six people and do it near a main street or a shopping center. Give each of the delegates twenty dollars and a list of five stores they must visit and allow them to choose one other as a "wild card."

Take them through the stuff in *Smart Retail* on:

▶ Reading stores

▶ Big Idea

▶ Mission and values

▶ Discovery

Then send them off, in teams of two, for two hours with the explicit brief that they must observe, talk to customers, and talk to staff. How they get those conversations going is up to them. They can play-act a bit if they want, whatever. But they must get those conversations going. They can spend their twenty dollars however they want to—a bit in each store, all at once, whatever.

The hard part

As well as making some specific observations (listed next), they will need to be taking note of everything with the idea to later apply this stuff to the creation of a sector-raiding Big Idea of their own.

Exercise

Part 1

On returning to the training room, we will be analyzing some of the retailers we've looked at against the following criteria:

▶ What is the Big Idea at each store?

▶ How does that translate into values (name five customer emotions per store)?

▶ How are they hanging these things together as part of the overall offer?

▶ What are they doing to create theater and discovery?

▶ What evidence can you cite supporting your views on Big Idea, values, and differentiation of each store?

Part 2

▶ How might you adapt each store to better suit the Big Idea?

▶ What might be a better Big Idea for each store?

Part 3

▶ As a group: Choose one market sector in which you think there might be room to try something new. Then find a Big Idea that would offer an opportunity for a new retail business in that sector.

Who would want to shop there?

Why?

What will the store look like?

How does discovery work in it?

What's the perfect customer experience going to feel like?

How will it compete?

What will it be called?

Run one of these sessions with your team and you will be stunned by what shakes out. Or get in touch with me and we can set one up and run it for you.

APPENDIX IV
Books for retailers

Decent books on retailing are few and far between, which is one of the reasons why I wrote this one. Of those rarities, the ones listed here are the best. Two of the titles are pretty hard to get hold of in the UK but are available at www.amazon.co.uk. Good bookshops may be able to order them for you too. I've marked the two in question with asterisks.

Visual Merchandising—Tony Morgan (Laurence King, 2008)

Absolutely essential retail reading—it's the one book on visual merchandising (windows, signage, fixtures, and fittings—if you're wondering) that manages to be both incredibly strong on the loveliness of design and on the practical things that design is there to support. A really good companion to *Smart Retail*. If you can afford it, get Tony's more recent book as well, concentrating on awesome window design: *Window Display: New Visual Merchandising* (Laurence King, 2010).

The Richer Way—Julian Richer (Richer Publishing, 5th edition, 2009)

Richer manages people better than anyone I have ever come across. This is the story of how he does that—essential reading.

Why We Buy—Paco Underhill (Simon & Schuster, updated and revised edition, 2009)

Retail anthropologist Underhill has an understanding of the habits of shopping that is just breathtaking. You have to read this if you're interested at all in customers—which you are.

People Don't Buy What You Sell: They Buy What You Stand For—Martin Butler with Simon Gravatt (Management Books 2000, 2005)

A brilliant combination of personal insight, powerful case studies, and loads of revealing interviews with star retailers. This one is another essential for all retailers.

Retail Success—George Whalin (Willoughby Press, 2001)*

George worked in a famous guitar store in 1960s California and has been a leading retail mind ever since. He told me that the moment he realized that he wanted to be a retailer was the first time he sold a customer a guitar package that made both him and the customer smile. I love that.

See, Feel, Think, Do—**Andy Milligan and Shaun Smith (Marshall Cavendish, new edition, 2008)**

A brilliant book about learning to trust your instincts and to become more proactive in your decision-making. Loads of retail case studies; brilliant instinctive retailer Jane Shepherdson says it best in her endorsement for this book: "The sooner we start acting on our instincts, and listening less to business school theories, the more the customer will benefit." This book will help you to do that better, more often.

Made in America: My Story—**Sam Walton with John Huey (Doubleday, 1992)***

The story of how Sam Walton and his team built the world's biggest company: Wal-Mart. This is a lot of fun, full of breathtaking daring, down-home philosophy, and some great retail stories. An absolute must-read, even now so long after it was first published. I love this book.

Index

measurement trap 77–9
and you 82–4
impulse buying 169, 185–6
incentives, demotivating 68
information sharing 65
Internet xii-xiii
marketing 137–40
resources 83

JCDecaux 141
JFDI management style 49–50
job descriptions and fun 45–6
John Lewis Partnership 157

kaizen 75
Kamprad, Ingvar 198–200
KFC and recognition 57, 58–9
Krispy Kreme doughnuts 174–5
Kroc, Ray 53

leadership 36–7
Leahy, Sir Terry 103
Leonard, Stew 163–5
Les Nereides jewelry 170–1
listening 66, 83
to customers 12, 19–20, 81
to store staff 12, 13
Livengood, Scott 174
local press 127, 128
local radio broadcasts 129, 132
loyalty cards 104
loyalty, customer 40, 41, 104
loyalty programs 125–6, 132
Lush body products 97, 118–19,
170
Big Idea 29, 163

mail-order, catalog-based 187
Malmaison hotel chain 170
management by fear 48, 49–50, 63
see also store managers
market traders 172, 173–4, 175,
177
history 189
marketing 135–47
catalogs 141–2

database 142–5
measuring effect of 145–7
online 137–40, 142–3
questions chain 137
radio and TV 140
Smartphone apps 139
strapline and Big Idea 25–6
Mast Brothers (NY, US) 176
Media Markt 31
Mellon Bank 102
merchandising 173–4
merchant dealing 115
mission 35–6, 41–6
mission statements 38, 41–2, 43,
75
and values 45, 46
mistakes 52–3, 84
admitting 68, 95
Kamprad on 199–200
motivation of team 61–73
components of 61
financial reward 62–3
implied sanction 63–4
measuring 63
non-financial rewards 68–72
and recognition 53, 72
self-respect 64–8
movement and attention 168,
169–70
MPREIS store 28, 149
Myer (Adelaide, Australia) 98

Natural Grocery Company 103
needs of customers 109–11
glass exercise 110
my store exercise 111
shirt exercise 110
non-financial rewards 68–72
balloon day 71–2
team ballot 71

observable positive behaviors 56,
57, 72
observing
customers 16–17
store components 17–18